Great Robberies

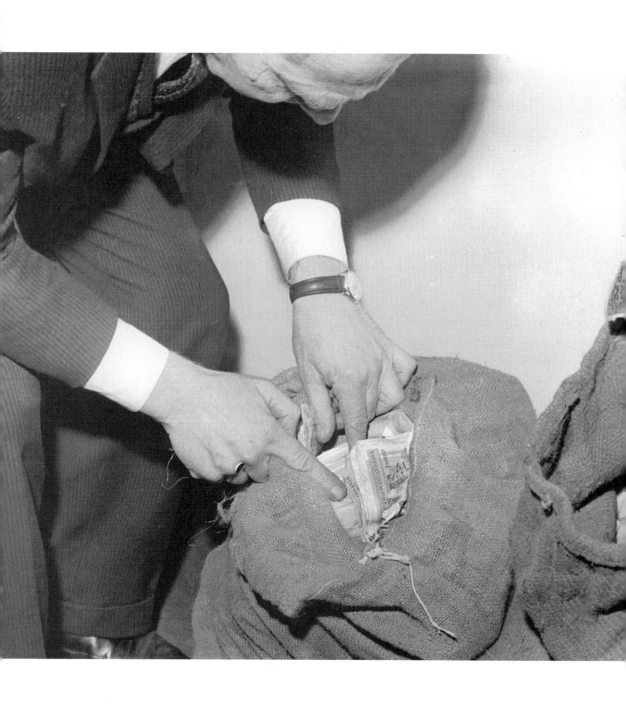

CRIME, JUSTICE, AND PUNISHMENT

Great Robberies

Richard Worth

Austin Sarat, GENERAL EDITOR

CHELSEA HOUSE PUBLISHERS
Philadelphia

Frontispiece: *Detectives examine sacks of currency stolen during England's "great train robbery" of 1963.*

Chelsea House Publishers

Production Manager Pamela Loos
Art Director Sara Davis
Director of Photography Judy L. Hasday
Managing Editor James D. Gallagher
Senior Production Editor J. Christopher Higgins

Staff for GREAT ROBBERIES

Senior Editor John Ziff
Associate Art Director/Designer Takeshi Takahashi
Picture Researcher Sandy Jones
Cover Designer Takeshi Takahashi

First Printing

1 3 5 7 9 8 6 4 2

The Chelsea House World Wide Web address is
http://www.chelseahouse.com

Library of Congress Cataloging-in-Publication Data

Worth, Richard.
Great robberies: crime, justice, and punishment / Richard
Worth.
  p. cm.
Includes bibliographical references and index.

ISBN 0-7910-4265-0

1. Robbery—History—Juvenile literature. 2. Bank
robberies—History—Juvenile literature. 3. Art thefts—
History—Juvenile literature. [1. Robbers and Outlaws.
2. Art thefts.] I. Title.

HV6648.W67 2000
364.15'52—dc21
00-031564

Contents

CRIME, JUSTICE, AND PUNISHMENT

Fears and Fascinations:

An Introduction to Crime, Justice, and Punishment

By Austin Sarat

We live with crime and images of crime all around us. Crime evokes in most of us a deep aversion, a feeling of profound vulnerability, but it also evokes an equally deep fascination. Today, in major American cities the fear of crime is a major fact of life, some would say a disproportionate response to the realities of crime. Yet the fear of crime is real, palpable in the quickened steps and furtive glances of people walking down darkened streets. At the same time, we eagerly follow crime stories on television and in movies. We watch with a "who done it" curiosity, eager to see the illicit deed done, the investigation undertaken, the miscreant brought to justice and given his just deserts. On the streets the presence of crime is a reminder of our own vulnerability and the precariousness of our taken-for-granted rights and freedoms. On television and in the movies the crime story gives us a chance to probe our own darker motives, to ask "Is there a criminal within?" as well as to feel the collective satisfaction of seeing justice done.

Fear and fascination, these two poles of our engagement with crime, are, of course, only part of the story. Crime is, after all, a major social and legal problem, not just an issue of our individual psychology. Politicians today use our fear of, and fascination with, crime for political advantage. How we respond to crime, as well as to the political uses of the crime issue, tells us a lot about who we are as a people as well as what we value and what we tolerate. Is our response compassionate or severe? Do we seek to understand or to punish, to enact an angry vengeance or to rehabilitate and welcome the criminal back into our midst? The CRIME, JUSTICE, AND PUNISHMENT series is designed to explore these themes, to ask why we are fearful and fascinated, to probe the meanings and motivations of crimes and criminals and of our responses to them, and, finally, to ask what we can learn about ourselves and the society in which we live by examining our responses to crime.

Crime is always a challenge to the prevailing normative order and a test of the values and commitments of law-abiding people. It is sometimes a Raskolnikov-like act of defiance, an assertion of the unwillingness of some to live according to the rules of conduct laid out by organized society. In this sense, crime marks the limits of the law and reminds us of law's all-too-regular failures. Yet sometimes there is more desperation than defiance in criminal acts; sometimes they signal a deep pathology or need in the criminal. To confront crime is thus also to come face-to-face with the reality of social difference, of class privilege and extreme deprivation, of race and racism, of children neglected, abandoned, or abused whose response is to enact on others what they have experienced themselves. And occasionally crime, or what is labeled a criminal act, represents a call for justice, an appeal to a higher moral order against the inadequacies of existing law.

Figuring out the meaning of crime and the motivations of criminals and whether crime arises from defiance, desperation, or the appeal for justice is never an easy task. The motivations and meanings of crime are as varied as are the persons who engage in criminal conduct. They are as mysterious as any of the mysteries of the human soul. Yet the desire to know the secrets of crime and the criminal is a strong one, for in that knowledge may lie one step on the road to protection, if not an assurance of one's own personal safety. Nonetheless, as strong as that desire may be, there is no available technology that can allow us to know the whys of crime with much confidence, let alone a scientific certainty. We can, however, capture something about crime by studying the defiance, desperation, and quest for justice that may be associated with it. Books in the CRIME, JUSTICE, AND PUNISHMENT series will take up that challenge. They tell stories of crime and criminals, some famous, most not, some glamorous and exciting, most mundane and commonplace.

This series will, in addition, take a sober look at American criminal justice, at the procedures through which we investigate crimes and identify criminals, at the institutions in which innocence or guilt is determined. In these procedures and institutions we confront the thrill of the chase as well as the challenge of protecting the rights of those who defy our laws. It is through the efficiency and dedication of law enforcement that we might capture the criminal; it is in the rare instances of their corruption or brutality that we feel perhaps our deepest betrayal. Police, prosecutors, defense lawyers, judges, and jurors administer criminal justice and in their daily actions give substance to the guarantees of the Bill of Rights. What is an adversarial system of justice? How does it work? Why do we have it? Books in the CRIME, JUSTICE, AND PUNISHMENT series will examine the thrill of the chase as we seek to capture the criminal. They will also reveal the drama and majesty of the criminal trial as well as the day-to-day reality of a criminal justice system in which trials are the exception and negotiated pleas of guilty are the rule.

When the trial is over or the plea has been entered, when we have separated the innocent from the guilty, the moment of punishment has arrived. The injunction to punish the guilty, to respond to pain inflicted by inflicting pain, is as old as civilization itself. "An eye for an eye and a tooth for a tooth" is a biblical reminder that punishment must measure pain for pain. But our response to the criminal must be better than and different from the crime itself. The biblical admonition, along with the constitutional prohibition of "cruel and unusual punishment," signals that we seek to punish justly and to be just not only in the determination of who can and should be punished, but in how we punish as well. But neither reminder tells us what to do with the wrongdoer. Do we rape the rapist, or burn the home of the arsonist? Surely justice and decency say no. But, if not, then how can and should we punish? In a world in which punishment is neither identical to the crime nor an automatic response to it, choices must be made and we must make them. Books in the CRIME, JUSTICE, AND PUNISHMENT series will examine those choices and the practices, and politics, of punishment. How do we punish and why do we punish as we do? What can we learn about the rationality and appropriateness of today's responses to crime by examining our past and its responses? What works? Is there, and can there be, a just measure of pain?

CRIME, JUSTICE, AND PUNISHMENT brings together books on some of the great themes of human social life. The books in this series capture our fear and fascination with crime and examine our responses to it. They remind us of the deadly seriousness of these subjects. They bring together themes in law, literature, and popular culture to challenge us to think again, to think anew, about subjects that go to the heart of who we are and how we can and will live together.

*   *   *   *   *

Great crimes take great planning. Great crimes also display high drama. While it seems counterintuitive to talk about crimes by labeling some "great," that label here only refers to the elements of planning and drama. Crimes, whether robberies or other crimes, are not great in a moral sense. By definition, they cannot be, at least not in a just legal order.

This fascinating book presents a series of compelling case studies of great robberies. The robberies span history, and, in one sense, each is a story about the epoch in which it occurred. This book tells us about the characters who planned and carried out these crimes, about their motives, and about their strategies. It gives readers an inside account of lives dedicated to one great "score" and of the processes through which the perpetrators of great robberies are brought to justice. In so doing, this book makes great issues of crime and justice come alive.

Preface

Five or six times every minute, according to crime statistics gathered by the federal government, someone in the United States burglarizes a residence or other building or robs another person face-to-face. In a typical year, American law enforcement officials make more than 450,000 arrests of criminals who have stolen, or have attempted to steal, cash or valuables in this manner. The vast majority of these thefts involve minimal planning and resourcefulness on the part of the perpetrator: a hoodlum pulls a handgun on the clerk at a convenience store and cleans out the cash drawer; a burglar breaks into a house while the residents are away and steals a TV, VCR, and CD player; a mugger snatches a woman's purse on a city street. In a society awash in crime, these kinds of thefts are so commonplace—and the robbers' methods so unremarkable—that many of us take notice only when we or someone we know is the victim.

In some cases, however, robbers set their sights considerably higher. Instead of stealing $100 from a convenience store, they may try to steal $100,000 from a bank; instead of breaking into a home to take some electronics, they may break into a museum to take some priceless paintings. In these cases we are more apt to take notice—indeed, our interest seems directly proportional to the amount the robbers steal. In fact, when the amount taken in a robbery is sufficiently large, we sometimes call it a "great" robbery.

But besides the amount of the haul, is a great robbery fundamentally any different from a petty one? In some ways, the answer is yes. Clearly security at a major bank or art museum will be greater than security at the typical residence, because the bank and the museum stand to lose so much more than the home owner. A great robbery, then, requires more intelligence, planning, skill, and daring than an ordinary theft. The risks, like the potential rewards, are much larger.

The seven cases covered in this book, which include some of the most celebrated robberies in Europe and the United States during the 19th and 20th centuries, demonstrate both major aspects of a great robbery: the large size of the potential rewards and the unusual qualities of the thieves and their crimes. In one case, the robber broke new criminal ground, pulling off the first known theft of a famous painting from a museum or art gallery, in 1876. That criminal mastermind, Adam Worth, showed the way for generations of crooks to come, including two as-yet-unidentified men who in March 1990 stole artwork valued at $300 million from the Isabella Stewart Gardner Museum in Boston. In another case discussed in this book, a gang of British thieves also looked to the past for criminal inspiration, but in a surprising way. In 1963, these thieves resurrected a type of robbery that most people thought had disappeared at the end of the previous century: train robbery. Recognizing a unique opportunity, the thieves robbed a special mail train of the equivalent of more than $7 million. That amount, while impressive, pales in comparison with what thieves seized in 1945, when another unique opportunity presented itself. In the chaotic days leading up to and immediately following the defeat of Nazi Germany in World War II, cash and gold estimated to be worth $400 million was plundered from Germany's central bank.

An interesting question arises from a close examination of these and other great robberies: What, if anything, can be said about the character and motivations of the people who carried them out? The answers may not be as obvious as one might think. Of course, anyone who commits a robbery of any size is, by definition, willing to break the law for material gain, whether out of need or out of greed. But the perpetrator of a great robbery is much more likely than the petty criminal to have a range of legitimate options for material success, precisely because the qualities needed to pull off a great robbery—cleverness, intelligence, the ability to plan, attention to detail, boldness—are qualities that law-abiding society also tends to reward.

A celebrated (though fictitious) story is told about Willie Sutton, a famous robber and prison escape artist. "Why do you rob banks?" a journalist supposedly asked Sutton. "Because that's where the money is," Sutton is said to have replied. Though it was actually made up by a newspaper reporter, the exchange nevertheless seems to illustrate the difference between the law-abiding citizen and the robber, who feels no need to explain or justify his illegal activities but simply reduces the issue to a practical question: where is the best place to steal the money he desires? In his memoir *Where the Money Was*, Sutton—who robbed about 100 banks during his long criminal career—revealed that his actual motivations amounted to a lot more than simply greed: "Why did I rob banks? Because I enjoyed it. I loved it. I was more alive when I was inside a bank, robbing it, than at any other time in my life. I enjoyed everything about it so much that one or two weeks later I'd be looking for the next job. But to me the money was the chips, that's all."

Similar motivations seem to have been shared by several of the criminals whose robberies are examined in this book. Jesse James, for example, made plenty of money during his fabled career as an outlaw and could have settled into a life of farming or ranching with the wife and children all sources say he genuinely adored.

Indeed, for several years after the disastrous Northfield bank robbery chronicled in this book, James did retire from crime, but he clearly missed the excitement and challenge of robbing banks and trains. And there is no doubt he also enjoyed his celebrity: rather than trying to conceal his identity, he took to telling his victims who he was, and sometimes he even wrote descriptions of his crimes for the press. Likewise, at several points in his career, criminal mastermind Adam Worth could have retired and lived a comfortable, respectable life with the money he had made from his robberies and various other capers. Yet Worth was continually drawn back into crime by the excitement and thrill of it. By the late 1940s Anthony Pino and his gang had stolen more than half a million dollars, and the police had no evidence tying them to any crime. Yet like Adam Worth and Jesse James, Pino couldn't let go of his criminal ways. He dreamed of a monumental heist that would cap his career. That heist turned out to be the famous 1950 Brink's robbery. As these stories demonstrate, while the desire for money and the things it can buy obviously plays a large role in the motivations of great robbers, greed is often only part of the explanation.

Great robberies, and the way we view them, also say something interesting about society. Beyond the understandable fascination with how these crimes are committed, there is a strong tendency to glamorize great robberies, which are frequently depicted in fictional and fact-based books and motion pictures. What's more, the (mostly law-abiding) public that reads and watches these entertaining stories often ends up sympathizing with—even rooting for—the lawbreakers. The sympathetic, even comic, treatment of Anthony Pino's gang in the 1978 film *The Brink's Job* is but one case in point. A century earlier, Jesse James was lionized for his criminal exploits. Countless newspaper stories, magazine articles, and dime novels depicted him—with little or no basis in fact—as a courageous modern-day

Robin Hood, stealing from the rich and generally fighting injustice. Ignored was his very real propensity for cold-blooded murder.

Various factors may explain why we tend to romanticize the great robber in a way we certainly don't the common hood. First of all, the dream of reaping a huge financial windfall—the goal of any great robbery—has almost universal appeal. Perpetrators of great robberies get rich by relying on their wits and nerve, and they risk paying a heavy price should these qualities be found lacking. That, too, has a certain appeal in a society with a tradition of rugged individualism.

Perhaps the vastly different way we view the perpetrators of great robberies and the perpetrators of petty thefts also has something to do with the perceived victims. The petty criminal typically targets individuals. All of us are vulnerable to having our money or property stolen by this sort of hoodlum. And not only that, encounters with robbers frequently turn violent, so there is reason to be concerned about our personal safety. The perpetrator of a great robbery, on the other hand, is likely to target an institution—a bank, a museum, a large business—because, in the attributed words of Willie Sutton, that's where the money is. When the victim of a robbery is an institution, and particularly when no one is injured in the heist, many of us have a tendency to downplay the harm done. After all, insurance will probably cover the losses, and even if it doesn't, institutions have deep pockets. They can afford an occasional setback, we reason.

In reality, while we may not be affected personally, we are all indirect victims of great robberies. The money stolen from a bank must be replaced by the government at taxpayers' expense. The great painting taken from a museum can't be viewed and enjoyed by the public. But most important, perhaps, the great robbery—like crime of all types—undermines respect for the law. Our tolerance for great robbers is indeed misplaced.

STEALING THE DUCHESS

"He is the Napoleon of crime . . . ," Sherlock Holmes tells his loyal sidekick, Dr. Watson. "He is the organizer of half that is evil and of nearly all that is undetected in this great city." Holmes is referring to his archenemy, Professor Moriarty—an evil genius who matches wits with the great detective in a series of short stories penned in the late 19th century by the English author Sir Arthur Conan Doyle.

Doyle did not create the character of Moriarty out of whole cloth. His fictional portrait of London's most nefarious criminal was based on the life and times of a real master thief: Adam Worth, alias Henry Raymond. Worth, one of the world's great crime bosses, planned daring robberies throughout Europe and America, then sent his henchmen to carry them out. But in perhaps his most daring and famous heist, Worth himself did the dirty work. In 1876, he stole one of England's most valuable paintings: *Georgiana, Duchess of Devonshire*,

Georgiana, Duchess of Devonshire, *by the English artist Thomas Gainsborough. Master thief Adam Worth stole the painting in the hopes that he could use it to obtain his brother's release from jail.*

the portrait of an extraordinarily beautiful woman.

Worth's career in crime had begun many years earlier, while he was still a teenager. Born in Germany around 1845, he was raised in Cambridge, Massachusetts, after his parents immigrated to the United States. His family was quite poor, and at the age of 14 Worth decided to run away from home to seek his fortune in New York City. He had barely begun working as a clerk when the Civil War broke out. Worth enlisted in the Union army. Later he deserted his unit and signed up with another—an illegal practice that he would repeat over and over, each time receiving a bounty payment for enlisting. Worth finally left the army for good and returned to New York—not to become a clerk again, but to make crime his full-time profession.

By the mid-1860s, New York was America's biggest city, with a population of more than 800,000. It was a place of enormous contrasts. While it contained large areas of poverty where new immigrants, especially from Ireland and Germany, lived in rickety tenement buildings, New York also boasted glittering mansions that housed the wealthy. Many New Yorkers had grown prosperous running fashionable stores, owning ships that sailed out of the city's harbor, and selling supplies to the Union army during the war. These well-to-do New Yorkers were often easy prey for the estimated 30,000 thieves who lived and plied their trade in the city.

Worth joined this large group of robbers as a pickpocket—the lowest rung on the ladder of crime. He dreamed of becoming rich and believed that thievery was the surest path to this goal; honest people with his background generally ended up working long hours in a store or factory for very little money. Known as "Little Adam" because of his small size, Worth nevertheless seemed to possess a natural talent for leadership, and in a short time he had several other pickpockets working for him. Often they operated together: One pickpocket

One of the few known photos of Adam Worth.

would bump a victim on a crowded street. A second thief would use this distraction to steal the victim's watch or wallet, which he passed to a third member of the team, who quickly escaped with the stolen items.

In 1864, Worth was arrested and jailed in the large New York prison at Sing Sing. But he soon escaped by hiding in a drainage ditch. The short stint behind bars had taught the young criminal a lesson, however. For the same risks he would do far better by moving into more lucrative areas of crime, such as bank robbery.

Unfortunately, in the New York underworld of the day, Worth needed to be introduced to the top criminals before he would be asked to participate in a major crime. His big break came when he met Fredericka "Marm" Mandelbaum, a 250-pound woman considered the city's reigning queen of crime. Mandelbaum was a highly successful "fence," meaning that she resold stolen goods such as jewelry or bonds without the items being traced back to the criminals who pilfered them. Her criminal connections helped Worth move up to the next level in the criminal world.

Soon Little Adam was participating in the holdup of a bank in his old hometown of Cambridge. The heist netted him bonds valued at $20,000, which Marm Mandelbaum fenced. More important, Mandelbaum introduced Worth to Charles W. "Piano Charley" Bullard, a talented musician and notorious safecracker. Together, the two robbed the Boylston National Bank of Boston in 1869, escaping with an estimated $200,000. This sum, considerable even by today's standards, at the time constituted a huge haul—so huge, in fact, that Bullard and Worth feared that the police would work tirelessly to solve the case. So they decided to leave the country and live in England under assumed names. Adam Worth took on a new identity as a wealthy merchant banker named Henry J. Raymond.

But that didn't mean he had decided to go straight. Over the next few years, Worth was involved in various illegal activities. He robbed a large pawnshop in Liverpool, England, and opened the American Bar in Paris, where he ran an illegal gambling operation. The American Bar soon became a popular gathering place where notorious criminals drank, gambled, and planned new crimes.

The bar also attracted the attention of one of the world's best-known detectives, William Pinkerton. The son of Allan Pinkerton—founder of the Pinkerton National Detective Agency—the burly, 200-pound sleuth traveled to Worth's establishment during his pursuit of American bank robbers who had fled the

Charles W. "Piano Charley" Bullard, skilled at both music and safecracking, joined Worth in the 1869 robbery of the Boylston National Bank of Boston.

country. The Pinkerton agency, headquartered in Chicago, had also been retained to track down the thieves who had robbed the Boylston bank. Pinkerton knew the American Bar was a lucrative front for illegal operations. So did the French police, who began raiding the bar and eventually closed down the gambling tables, forcing Worth to return to England in 1875.

Worth had made enough money in Paris that he could afford to buy a lavish home in London and entertain Britain's wealthy aristocrats, who had no idea that the financier Henry Raymond was really a master thief. Worth was proud of his success and enjoyed living in luxury.

Worth's accomplices in the theft of the Duchess. This page: Little Joe Elliott. Facing page: Jack "Junka" Phillips, in what the Pinkerton detectives who captured him quaintly referred to as an "unwilling photograph."

In order to maintain his extravagant lifestyle, however, he continued pulling off robberies. Like the fictional Professor Moriarty, he carefully designed each caper, then the plan was mysteriously delivered to a team of thieves who didn't even know who was in charge of the robbery. In this way, Worth maintained his secret identity and shielded himself from the law should one of his plans go awry. Nevertheless, the Pinkertons kept an eye on his activities from America, and Scotland Yard—London's famous police force— suspected that Worth was the mastermind behind many unsolved crimes.

One of Worth's most lucrative activities was a counterfeiting ring that passed hundreds of thousands of dollars' worth of fraudulent bank-notes throughout Europe. Worth had involved his brother John, a petty thief, in the operation—and eventually that would create a problem. John Worth was arrested in France and ultimately sent back to England, where he was wanted by Scotland Yard.

Adam Worth was fiercely loyal to all the men who worked for him. If they were arrested, he did whatever he could to get them released, including paying huge bribes to the police. And in this case it was his own brother who was facing a long prison sentence. But John's release would take more than hefty bribes. Worth devised an even more daring scheme—one that involved the famous portrait of the duchess of Devonshire.

Georgiana Spencer, who had married the duke of Devonshire in 1774, was considered among the most beautiful women of her era. In 1787, she posed for a portrait by Thomas Gainsborough, one of England's greatest artists, who had already painted her twice. Soon after this portrait was completed, however, it disappeared. The painting resurfaced during the 1840s and was purchased by a wealthy merchant. When he died in 1875, the painting was put up for sale by Christie's, a prominent London auction house. In the days leading up to the May 1876 auction, the painting created quite a stir in London. Thousands of people filed into Christie's to see the image of this beautiful woman, who had led a life surrounded by scandal. It was the 19th-century version of a media event, though the center of all the attention had been dead for almost 75 years.

The publicity probably didn't hurt the selling price. At the auction, William Agnew, the owner of a London art gallery, bought the painting for over $50,000—the equivalent of more than $600,000 today. No one had ever paid this much for a painting.

Agnew put the picture on display in his gallery, charging an admission fee for people who wanted to view it. One of these people was Adam Worth. His interest in the Duchess extended beyond appreciation of great art: the master thief had decided to steal the painting, not only because he liked the challenge of carrying out such a great heist, but also because he believed he could use the painting to bargain for his brother's release. After stealing the Duchess, he planned to contact Agnew anonymously and offer to return the painting if the art dealer agreed to put up a bail bond to get John out of jail. In England in those days, bonds were accepted only from people of prominence, like Agnew. Once the bond had been received and John was released, he would flee the country.

Worth planned the theft for the night of May 25, 1876. It was a foggy evening, with only the soft glow of gaslights illuminating London's dark streets. Worth approached Agnew's gallery with two other men, Jack "Junka" Phillips, his huge bodyguard, and Little Joe Elliott, a member of Worth's forgery ring. Leaving Elliott on the street corner to keep an eye out for the police, Worth and Phillips walked to the front of the gallery. Phillips lifted his much smaller boss up to the second floor, where the Gainsborough was displayed, and Worth pried open the window with a crowbar. Sneaking into the gallery, he carefully cut the painting out of its frame with his knife, rolled it up, and put the picture under his coat, then exited as he had entered—through the window. A few moments later, the three thieves were leaving the scene of the crime.

When the theft was discovered, it immediately became one of the most celebrated crimes of the century. Scotland Yard sent out descriptions of the painting to police forces throughout the world, because no one knew who had stolen the painting or where they might have taken it. The duchess is "dressed in white," Scotland Yard explained, "with a blue silk petticoat and sash, and a large black hat and feathers. She is turned three-quarters to the right, the eyes directed toward the spectator, the hair profusely curled, powdered and falling upon the shoulders; the complexion is very brilliant, and the arms folded across the waist."

As the giant police hunt proceeded, however, John Worth was unexpectedly freed from prison on a technicality—rendering unnecessary his brother's plan to obtain his release with the portrait. Unable to sell the painting without drawing suspicion on himself, Worth decided to leave England and sail for the United States.

Worth let the publicity over the theft die down a bit before he made his next move. In December, William Agnew received a letter from someone offering to return the picture for $15,000 in gold. It was signed "New York." Enclosed with the letter was a piece of the canvas that had been hidden by the frame. The writer instructed Agnew to put a small advertisement in the *London Times* if he was interested in making a deal. On January 2, an ad appeared that said: "New York, Letter received. On further proof are prepared to treat."

Soon Agnew received another letter, along with a larger piece of the picture. He was now prepared to make a deal. The mysterious "New York"—who was, of course, Adam Worth—then wrote Agnew that he was sending a representative to London to contact the art dealer. But no representative ever appeared. Finally, Agnew received another letter. Worth had changed his mind and wanted Agnew to send someone to America to make the deal. Agnew refused. In August, Worth sent another letter saying that a deal could be made in London. But no deal was ever made, Worth apparently deciding he might be caught by the police. *Georgiana, Duchess of Devonshire* had disappeared again.

Worth had the painting safely hidden away while he engaged in other robberies. There was a daring diamond theft in South Africa in 1880, another holdup at a London post office the following year, and a bank robbery in California a few years later. While he was in the United States, Worth had stashed the painting in a Boston warehouse where no one would look for it. Meanwhile, he continued to play the role of Henry Raymond, his true identity remaining a secret even to his wife and two children. In 1892, Worth traveled to Liège, Belgium, where he orchestrated the robbery of a vehicle that delivered cash to various banks in the city.

While making his escape, however, Worth was caught by the police. After a lengthy interrogation, he was finally brought to trial, convicted of burglary, and sentenced to seven years in prison. The entire affair came as such a shock to his wife, who had thought she was married to a respectable businessman, that she began drinking heavily and later went insane. Worth's children were sent to America, where they lived with his brother John.

Although he served only about four years of his sentence, Worth suffered terribly in prison. After his release, he planned new robberies, but his energy and leadership as a crime boss were depleted. As his health deteriorated, he seemed eager to take care of one important piece of unfinished business—the famous painting of the duchess of Devonshire. Worth wanted to return the painting, but without being prosecuted for the robbery. He also hoped to receive a reward that he might use to help support his children.

Worth could not risk making a deal himself. He needed an intermediary with certain special qualities: a

spotless reputation, so Agnew would trust him to deliver the painting; the discretion to keep Worth's name out of the entire negotiations; and enough stature in the police world to prevent Scotland Yard from pursuing the man who had stolen the painting. One person with all of these qualifications was William Pinkerton.

Over the years, Pinkerton had developed an unusual reputation among the world's great thieves. Known as "the Eye"—which was also the symbol of his detective agency—Pinkerton was considered a tireless foe of crime who would stop at almost nothing to capture a criminal. On the other hand, he also liked to go to bars where thieves hung out and had even developed

Fabled detective William Pinkerton in his Chicago office. Pinkerton's stature among both law enforcement agents and lawbreakers made him the ideal intermediary for the return of the Duchess.

close relationships with some of them. Indeed, he had enormous respect for certain criminals, whom he regarded as masters of their craft. Chief among them was Adam Worth, whose exploits Pinkerton had followed for three decades.

In 1899, Worth sent a telegram to Pinkerton's office in Chicago. It read: "Letter awaiting you at house; send for it." The telegram was signed "Roy." The letter said that there was a "matter that might be to our mutual benefit," but the writer asked for a guarantee that "no advantage will be taken of my position, and that no use will ever be made of any information." If Pinkerton agreed, he was to put an advertisement in the *Chicago Daily News*. Pinkerton placed the ad, which said: "ASSURANCE GIVEN—W.A.P." The next day Worth met Pinkerton at his office. The two men talked on and off for three days, not only about the Gainsborough painting, but also about Worth's other criminal exploits. Eventually, they made a deal.

Pinkerton communicated with Scotland Yard, without mentioning Worth's name. The Yard, in turn, assured the Agnew gallery that the deal was genuine. Negotiations continued for many months over how much should be paid for the painting and where the final transfer would take place. Finally, C. Morland Agnew, the son of the gallery's founder, agreed to travel to Chicago with the reward money. Agnew met Pinkerton, and the two men waited in a hotel room for the painting to be delivered. Eventually, a messenger arrived with a rolled-up canvas. After he had left, Agnew carefully examined the painting. He smiled with relief—it was the genuine Gainsborough.

Agnew returned to London in 1901 with the Duchess, and when he put it on display in his art gallery, thousands of people flocked to see it. But the painting remained in England only for a short time. It was purchased for $150,000 by the wealthy American financier John Pierpont Morgan, who added the Gainsborough to his vast art collection. Shortly afterward, Worth, already seriously ill when the painting was returned, died.

William Pinkerton, who had greatly admired Worth, later wrote an article about the thief's long career. As Pinkerton put it: "I consider this man the most remarkable criminal of his day."

THE NORTHFIELD BANK ROBBERY

T he same year that Adam Worth stole the magnificent portrait *Georgiana, Duchess of Devonshire* in London, another great robbery took place across the Atlantic Ocean, in the small town of Northfield, Minnesota. If Worth preferred to work behind the scenes, meticulously planning crimes that others carried out for him, the leader of the Northfield robbers, who reveled in the publicity his heists created, has probably never been surpassed for sheer audacity. Although Worth may have been, as William Pinkerton suggested, "the most remarkable criminal of his day," his identity remained virtually unknown to all but a select group of professional lawmen. By contrast, the outlaw who struck Northfield on the morning of September 7, 1876, was not only widely known, but also widely viewed as a hero. Indeed, to this day he

Northfield, Minnesota, circa 1870. The First National Bank, the James gang's intended target, is the building with arches at right.

retains an almost mythic status, and his exploits have been celebrated in song, in stories, and in motion pictures. His name was Jesse James.

For an entire decade, the notorious James gang had robbed banks, trains, and an occasional stagecoach in the frontier regions of the American West, stealing more than $200,000 and, despite being the most wanted outlaws in the country, never once suffering a major setback. Ironically, the gang's most famous holdup—the Northfield bank robbery—was the only one in which they got away with absolutely nothing. What's more, the disastrous raid marked the downfall of the James gang.

The long trail that led to Northfield began during the early 1840s, when Robert James and his wife, Zerelda, moved to Missouri. The Jameses were part of the great pioneer migration that flowed across the Mississippi River during the mid-19th century, when thousands of Americans headed west to establish new homesteads. In 1843, Zerelda gave birth to a son named Alexander Franklin, who would be known throughout his life as Frank; four years later a second son, Jesse, was born.

Robert James did not succeed in Missouri as he had hoped. In 1850, he headed for the recently discovered goldfields of California, leaving behind his wife and young children while he sought his fortune as a prospector. Soon, however, he contracted pneumonia and died, never having found the gold he'd dreamed of. His widow Zerelda eventually married Dr. Reuben Samuel, who helped raise Frank and Jesse and with whom she had four additional children.

As the James boys grew up, they counted among their close friends the sons of a well-to-do landowner named Henry Younger. Four of these brothers—Cole, Jim, John, and Bob Younger—would later ride with Jesse and Frank James in the gang that cut a swath of robbery and killing across the West.

To a certain extent the James and Younger brothers were products of their violent times. The so-called Middle Border region where they grew up was a harsh and wild place that abutted the unsettled Indian territories. In addition to the ordinary hardships of pioneer life, residents of the Border during the 1850s had to contend with increasing conflict over an issue that would eventually tear the nation apart: slavery.

In 1820, proslavery members of Congress from the South and abolitionists from the North had crafted the Missouri Compromise, whereby Maine was admitted to the Union as a free state and Missouri as a slave state, and slavery was prohibited in the remaining western territories north of Missouri's southern border. In the ensuing decades, as America grew increasingly polarized over the issue of slavery, the compromise helped maintain a fragile peace. In 1854, however, Congress passed the Kansas-Nebraska Act, which not only opened up Nebraska and Kansas to settlement, but also nullified key provisions of the Missouri Compromise. By the terms of the new legislation, popular sovereignty—a vote by all residents—would determine whether Nebraska and Kansas became slave or free states.

Supporters and opponents of slavery raced to settle the territories. Although many Missourians moved west into neighboring Kansas, abolitionist settlers soon greatly outnumbered them. Slaveholders in Missouri organized armed groups, known as Border Ruffians, that rode into Kansas to burn farms and terrorize and murder abolitionist settlers. Kansans known as Jayhawkers formed their own units and struck back. The fighting was often savage, with atrocities committed by both sides, and soon the fate of "Bleeding Kansas" was pushing the entire country closer to civil war.

The James-Samuel family owned a few slaves and was very much in the proslavery camp. When the Civil War broke out in 1861, 18-year-old Frank James joined a militia unit formed to hold Missouri for the South. At

14, his brother, Jesse, was too young to fight. The pro-slavery militia was quickly routed by Union soldiers, however.

Like many militiamen, Frank James decided not to lay down his arms and instead joined one of the Confederate guerrilla bands harassing Union forces. Among Missourians of the Border region, hatred of the Union ran high—not only because a brutal military government had been clamped on their state, but also because regiments of Jayhawkers, thirsty for revenge for the Bleeding Kansas days, laid waste to much of western Missouri in the name of the Union cause.

Frank James and Cole Younger rode with one of the most infamous guerrilla leaders, William Clarke Quantrill. Quantrill's Raiders, as the bushwhackers were called, not only engaged in hit-and-run raids against Federal soldiers, but also burned and looted towns known to support the Union cause. In 1863, James and Younger participated in the terrible attack on Lawrence, Kansas, during which Quantrill and his men burned the town and wantonly massacred unarmed men and boys.

By 1864, Jesse James—now 17—and Jim Younger had also joined Quantrill's Raiders. Jesse rode with one of Quantrill's lieutenants, a particularly ruthless man known as Bloody Bill Anderson. Anderson had high praise for the young Jesse James. "Not to have any beard," the guerrilla leader said, "he is the keenest and cleanest fighter in the command." Jesse James participated with Anderson and his guerrillas in the vicious attack on Centralia, Kansas, in September 1864. Anderson's men shot up the town, robbed a stagecoach, then stopped an incoming train. Among the passengers were about 35 unarmed Union soldiers heading home on leave. The bushwhackers proceeded to execute and mutilate the Federal troops.

Later that year, Anderson's bushwhackers were themselves ambushed by Federal soldiers. Bloody Bill

Jesse James, age 17. By this time the angelic-looking farm boy from Missouri was a skilled and ruthless fighter with a Confederate guerrilla group.

and a number of his men were killed, but Jesse James managed to escape. In 1865, William Quantrill was killed, and Frank James, who was riding with him, surrendered.

In June of that year, with the war now over, Jesse James and a small group of bushwhackers attempted to surrender at Lexington, Missouri. Federal soldiers opened fire on them, however, and Jesse sustained a life-threatening chest wound from which it took him months to recover.

By the end of 1865, both Frank and Jesse James had returned to their family's ruined farm near Kearney,

Missouri. But the brothers did not settle easily into the life of farmers. Perhaps that was because they had seen—and committed—so much violence during the war. Perhaps they simply missed the excitement of living by their wits and their fighting skills. Or perhaps, as many supporters would suggest, the policies of the Radical Republican government that took power in Missouri after the Civil War, which discriminated against former Confederate fighters and sympathizers, drove the James boys to lawlessness.

On February 13, 1866, a group of former Confederate guerrillas rode into the town of Liberty, Missouri, headed for the Clay County Savings Bank, and carried out the first daylight bank robbery in U.S. history. The bandits took over $60,000 and killed a young college student on the street during their getaway. According to some reports, Frank James was one of the Liberty robbers; his brother, Jesse, almost certainly was not.

But Jesse James may well have been involved in a bank robbery in Lexington, Missouri, in October of the same year. And both James brothers, along with Cole, Jim, and Bob Younger, took part in a bank robbery in Richmond, Missouri, the following May. The heist turned deadly when townspeople tried to stop the bandits from making their escape. Richmond's mayor and a father and son were shot dead.

By 1868 the James brothers and Cole Younger had formed the core of the group that would be called the James-Younger gang, or simply the James gang. Aside from these three, the gang was surprisingly fluid, with different people—often Cole Younger's brothers, relatives of the Jameses, or men who had fought with them during the Civil War—participating in a robbery or two and then returning to quiet lives as farmers. In March 1868, three or four men joined Cole Younger and the James brothers in robbing a bank in Russellville, Kentucky. It was the first time the gang had struck outside the confines of their home state, and the

The Younger brothers (from left: Bob, Jim, and Cole), with their sister Henrietta. For nearly a decade the Youngers, childhood friends of the Jameses, robbed banks, trains, and an occasional stagecoach with the notorious James gang.

bandits netted a respectable $14,000.

Frank and Jesse James weren't as successful during their next robbery, which they carried out by themselves on December 7, 1869. The brothers got only $700 from the Daviess County Savings Bank in Gallatin, Missouri. But without provocation or warning, Jesse shot and killed the bank's owner and cashier, Captain John Sheets, apparently because he recognized Sheets as a former Union soldier who had been involved in the ambush that killed Bloody Bill Anderson. Outside the bank in Gallatin, Jesse's horse bolted, and the brothers

Jesse and Frank James were legends in their own time. Countless boys' magazines like the one shown here, dime novels, and newspaper stories depicted the outlaws as gallant heroes.

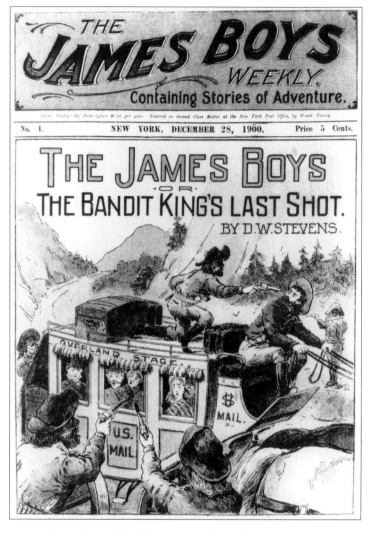

were forced to double up on Frank's mount to make their escape.

Unfortunately for the James brothers, Jesse's horse, an unusually fine specimen, was traced to its owner. A posse from Gallatin went to the Clay County farm of their mother and stepfather and surrounded the house. But the outlaws suddenly burst out of the barn on horseback, spurred their mounts over the barnyard fence, and made a daring escape with their guns blazing.

By the standards of the day, the James brothers'

guilt in the Daviess County Savings Bank robbery, and the murder of John Sheets, was more than adequately established. Plus, a substantial reward was offered for their capture. Yet no one did anything to help lawmen apprehend the bandits. In fact, neighbors in Clay County did their best to shield the brothers from justice—by providing alibis, lying about their where-abouts, and warning the Jameses when lawmen were in the area.

Conveniently ignoring the cold-blooded murders Frank and Jesse had committed, many Missourians considered the James brothers gallant heroes, loyal sons of the Confederacy who targeted Yankee-owned banks and businesses that, it was widely felt, were in league with Radical Republican politicians to exploit people with Southern sympathies. In the years after the Civil War, banks did foreclose on the farms of many Missourians. But there was little basis for the image that developed—within Missouri and throughout the country—of Jesse James as a latter-day Robin Hood who stole only from the rich.

Nonetheless, that image was reinforced by newspa-pers, particularly the *Kansas City Times*, whose editor, John Newman Edwards, had been a comrade in arms of the James brothers. Soon Jesse James himself was culti-vating his public image as a fun-loving, fearless, gallant bandit. On June 3, 1871, the citizens of Corydon, Iowa, had gathered in the town church to hear a speech by a well-known orator named Henry Clay Dean. Dean was telling them about the advantages of having a rail line run through their community, which, he said, would bring in more settlers and greater prosperity. Unknown to the townspeople, an event of much greater signifi-cance than Dean's oration was occurring a short dis-tance away. The James gang was holding up the local bank. The bank robbers heard about the town meeting, and after shoving $6,000 into their saddlebags, they rode over to the church. Jesse James dismounted, strode up to the podium, and coolly announced that the bank had just been robbed. The citizens of Corydon were stunned, but before they could do anything, the robbers had ridden away.

A little more than a year later, the gang struck the Kansas City State Fair in broad daylight. Jesse James put a gun to the head of the cashier and forced him to hand over $10,000 in receipts. As the bandits were escaping, a little girl was accidentally shot, but the sheer audacity shown by James in pulling off such a robbery caught the imagination of many people. One writer went so far as to compare James to a bold knight of King Arthur's Round Table. The real and imagined exploits of James and his gang were turned into dozens of dime novels and magazine articles, and stories about the robbers appeared in newspapers across America. James loved the attention and even began writing "press releases" describing his daring robberies, which he handed to his victims to turn over to newspapermen. Cole Younger got into the act during a stagecoach robbery in Hot Springs, Arkansas, when he made a grand show of returning the watch and money of a passenger after he found out the man had fought for the Confederacy during the Civil War.

In 1873, the James gang turned to train robbery. They were not the first thieves to hold up railroads, but they became famous for it. Their first target was the Chicago, Rock Island and Pacific Railroad, which they waylaid on a dark night in Iowa. The engineer was killed, and the robbers successfully looted money and jewelry from the frightened passengers. At the height of their success in 1874, the gang held up two stagecoaches, a bank, and two railroads over a wide area that included Kansas and Missouri, as well as Arkansas, Mississippi, and Texas.

When local law officials proved unable to stop the thieves, the Pinkerton National Detective Agency tried to capture them. In 1874, John Younger and two

Pinkerton agents were killed in a bloody shoot-out in Missouri. "I know that the James[es] and Youngers are desperate men," said Allan Pinkerton, the founder of the detective agency, "and that when we meet it must be the death of one or both of us."

Early in 1875, Pinkerton agents surrounded the Samuel farm, where they erroneously thought the James brothers were hiding. The Pinkertons threw a bomb into the house that killed the Samuels' young son, Archie, and severely wounded Mrs. Samuel. Public opinion turned strongly against the Pinkertons for this wanton act of violence, and there was even talk of indicting Allan Pinkerton for murder.

By this time the James gang seemed invincible. For nearly 10 years the gang had been committing daring and profitable robberies, and despite being pursued by lawmen, citizens' posses, and the world-famous Pinkertons, the core members had not suffered a major setback. Moreover, they enjoyed near-mythic status among the American public. All that would change when the gang decided to rob a bank in Minnesota, where one of the gang, Bill Chadwell (also known as William Stiles), used to live.

In addition to Chadwell, seven other bandits made the journey to Minnesota: Jesse and Frank James; Bob, Cole, and Jim Younger; Clell Miller; and Charlie Pitts. The gang members investigated a number of different locations in the North Star State but eventually settled on Northfield, a town of approximately 2,000 residents located on the eastern bank of the Cannon River about 40 miles south of St. Paul. There the First National Bank seemed ripe for the picking.

On the morning of September 7, 1876, the gang entered town in small groups. Jesse James, Bob Younger, and Charlie Pitts casually rode past the bank and then proceeded down the street to J. G. Jeft's restaurant, where they ate ham and eggs and made small talk with other patrons. After the meal, the three outlaws rode

This page: The First National Bank of Northfield as seen from the street. Opposite page: Interior of the bank. During the robbery, bank clerk A. E. Bunker attempted to lock Charlie Pitts in the vault at right.

back to the bank, where Cole Younger and Clell Miller now waited; Frank James, Jim Younger, and Bill Chadwell remained on the outskirts of town, in case there was any trouble. While Miller and Cole Younger guarded the door, Jesse James, Bob Younger, and Pitts entered the bank.

The robbery appeared to be going according to plan until hardware store owner J. S. Allen tried to go into the bank and was roughly turned away by Miller. Realizing what was happening, Allen immediately ran off and yelled, "Get your guns, boys. They are robbing the bank!" Cries of "Robbery! Robbery!" rang through the streets.

Miller and Cole Younger, trying to distract attention from the holdup in the bank, mounted their horses and rode through town shooting their pistols and killing a resident named Nicholas Gustavson. But Northfield's

residents weren't intimidated. They quickly got their guns and began firing at the outlaws. A medical student named Henry Wheeler took up position at a second-floor window of the Hotel Dampier; a businessman named A. B. Manning started firing across the street from the First National Bank.

Inside the bank, the bandits were encountering resistance as well. When one of the robbers held a knife to the throat of the cashier, J. L. Heywood, and demanded that he open the safe, Heywood responded, "There is a time lock on, and it cannot be opened now." When Pitts went to investigate this claim, the bank's clerk, A. E. Bunker, attempted to lock him in the vault. The thieves became so frustrated that one of them beat Heywood over the head with his pistol. Meanwhile, Bunker escaped through the rear of the bank, though Pitts managed to shoot him in the shoulder.

Soon the bandits inside the bank heard their comrades outside shouting for them to hurry up, and they decided to abandon the robbery attempt without getting a single dollar. But in a final act of senseless violence, one of them killed Heywood.

Out in the street, a pitched battle was raging. A Northfield resident named Elias Stacy had knocked Clell Miller off his horse with a shotgun blast of bird shot to the face. When Miller remounted and charged Stacy, medical student Henry Wheeler killed him with a shot from the hotel window. Store owner A. B. Manning took aim at Cole Younger, whom he seriously wounded in the shoulder. Then Manning pointed his rifle at Chadwell, who along with Frank James and Jim Younger had ridden in from the outskirts of town at the first sound of shooting. Manning's shot hit Chadwell in the chest and killed him instantly. Bob Younger, whose horse had been felled by a bullet, took up position behind a stack of boxes and traded fire with Manning until a shot by Wheeler shattered his elbow. Frank James was shot in the leg. Charlie Pitts and Jim Younger were also wounded.

Recognizing that they were defeated, the surviving members of the James gang beat a hasty retreat toward the Cannon River Bridge. When Cole Younger realized that they had left his brother Bob behind without a horse, he rode back through a hail of gunfire and hoisted Bob onto his mount.

The entire battle had taken about seven minutes. But in that short amount of time the residents of Northfield had decimated America's most infamous outlaw gang, making the Northfield robbery one of the most noteworthy in history.

Miller and Chadwell lay dead, but the gang's troubles were far from over. The residents of Northfield immediately formed a posse, and eventually hundreds of men from nearby communities joined in a massive manhunt. With everyone except Jesse James wounded,

Photo montage of some of the Northfield robbery protagonists. Cashier Joseph Heywood and outlaws Bill Chadwell and Clell Miller were killed the day of the robbery. Charlie Pitts died in a later gunfight with a posse, during which the Younger brothers were wounded and captured. Of the eight-man gang that rode into Northfield on September 7, only Frank and Jesse James escaped.

and with Cole and Bob Younger riding double, the gang couldn't move very fast. Plus, they were in unfamiliar territory, hundreds of miles from the friendly confines of western Missouri.

Soon the James brothers separated from the rest of the gang and headed into the Dakota Territory, where they forced a doctor to treat Frank James's leg wound. Then they headed toward Nebraska and disappeared.

The rest of the gang, however, was still trying to elude the posse, which chased them into a large forest before the thieves escaped. Then the outlaws made their way to an island in a swamp, and from there to an abandoned farmhouse. Unable to find the thieves, the posse was growing frustrated. Many had already given up the chase, believing that the members of the gang would outwit them, as they had so many other pursuers in the past.

Just as the trail seemed to turn cold and the search had almost ended, the gang members were spotted once more, this time near a lake southwest of Northfield. Clearly they had lost their way. A small group of men pursued them into the thick underbrush, where a fierce gunfight broke out. After a brief exchange of gunfire, the three Younger brothers—Bob, Cole, and Jim—were wounded and Pitts was killed. Finally, Bob Younger yelled out: "I surrender; they are all down but me."

The Youngers were taken into custody and stood trial for robbery and murder. Because they pled guilty, state law allowed their lives to be spared, but they were given life sentences in the Minnesota State Penitentiary. Bob died there in 1889. But in 1901, Cole and Jim were released because they had been model prisoners.

Meanwhile, the James brothers remained out of sight for a few years. Since there were no known photographs of the two brothers and the descriptions of them varied, it was almost impossible to identify them, making their capture even more difficult.

Frank took the alias B. J. Woodson and settled in

Nashville, Tennessee, with his young wife, Annie. Together they had a son in 1878. With the exception of a holdup in Muscle Shoals, Alabama, in 1881, Frank shunned his former outlaw ways.

Under the alias J. D. Howard, Jesse also settled in Nashville, where he and his wife, Zerelda, raised their son and daughter. But unlike his brother, Jesse grew restless and longed to return to a life of crime. In 1879, he formed a new gang, which robbed a Chicago and Alton Railroad train at Glendale, Missouri, taking about $6,000 from the express box. Over the next two years, the gang held up a stagecoach and two more railroads. In one of the robberies, they cruelly murdered the conductor and a passenger.

Because they had committed so many acts of violence, much of the support for the James brothers had finally eroded, but no one seemed resourceful or brave enough to capture them. In 1881, Missouri governor Thomas Crittenden finally convinced the railroad companies to put up a large reward—$10,000 apiece—for the capture and conviction of Jesse and Frank James.

Two of Jesse James's new gang members, Bob and Charlie Ford, decided that this was too much money to ignore. On April 3, 1882, they went to Jesse's house in St. Joseph, Missouri. After the three ate breakfast together, Bob Ford murdered Jesse by shooting him in the head while his back was turned.

Later that year Frank James surrendered to the authorities. He stood trial twice but was never convicted, and he slipped out of the public eye, drifting from one job to another. Then, in 1903, he went into partnership with Cole Younger, running a Wild West show with make-believe robberies. The show was unsuccessful, and James was forced to make a living selling tickets to people who wanted to see the famous Samuel family farm in Missouri. He died in 1915, a year before Cole Younger.

ROBBING THE REICHSBANK

By early 1945, Nazi Germany was in its death throes. The Third Reich, which dictator Adolf Hitler had predicted would endure for a thousand years, had lasted a mere 12. Earlier the vaunted German armed forces had come within a hairbreadth of conquering all of Europe, but now they were in retreat on two major fronts, fighting for their lives at the gates of the Fatherland. In the west, the Allies—led by the United States, Great Britain, and France—had pushed to the Rhine River and were poised for a final thrust into the heart of Germany. In the east, the Soviet Red Army had driven Hitler's troops all the way back into Poland, where Germany had first ignited World War II in 1939 with the surprise invasion of its neighbor.

Berlin, 1945: The ruined Chancellery, seat of Nazi Germany's government. The destruction and chaos accompanying the final days of World War II facilitated the plundering of Germany's central bank, considered the largest robbery in history.

As the Allies smashed the remnants of Hitler's once feared military, German civilians also paid an enormous price for their leader's failed dreams of domination. Supremacy in the air enabled the Allies to unleash a relentless bombing campaign that killed thousands of civilians, destroyed much of the country's infrastructure, and reduced many German cities to rubble. One soldier described the Allied aircraft as "droning like endless swarms of mad bumble bees." In February, almost 800 heavy bombers struck Dresden, creating an enormous firestorm that consumed the German city and killed more than 100,000 people. Allied aircraft also repeatedly bombed Berlin, the German capital. One huge daylight air raid during the winter of 1945 killed more than 2,000 Berliners and damaged the Chancellery, the center of the Nazi government.

In these desperate times, as the Third Reich moved ever closer to its final collapse, some people used the chaos and confusion to carry out what the *Guinness Book of Records* considers the biggest robbery in history: the looting of more than $400 million from Germany's central bank, the Reichsbank.

Actually, the plundering of the Reichsbank was accomplished not by a single stroke but by a series of separate acts, committed by various individuals and for a variety of reasons. But it all began in February of 1945, after an Allied air raid had severely damaged the Berlin headquarters of the Reichsbank. The central bank's president, Dr. Walther Funk, decided that the huge gold and cash reserves at the Reichsbank should be moved to safer quarters. So gold, currency, and other valuables worth more than $300 million were loaded on a railroad train and shipped southwest of Berlin to be hidden in a huge underground mine. Here, it was hoped, the great financial resources of Nazi Germany would be safe and could be used to continue financing the war effort.

Unfortunately for the Nazis, the mine was captured

only a few weeks later by advancing American armies. In addition to the transferred Reichsbank reserves and a large collection of magnificent paintings—which the Germans had looted from conquered countries during the early years of the war—the Americans found grisly reminders of the Nazis' program of genocide: sacks of diamonds and gold fillings taken from Jews murdered at the death camps.

In mid-April, the Soviets launched a heavy offensive on the German capital; the final, bloody battle for Berlin had begun. "As far as I could see," one German soldier later recalled, "the sky was a gold-red, fires of assorted sizes were burning everywhere, the sound of several thousand Russian artillery . . . was one endless clap and roll of terrifying thunder and lightning. . . ."

Retreating to his concrete bunker under the streets of Berlin, Adolf Hitler continued to direct what was left of the German war effort. Sick, exhausted, and, according to one of his associates, a "senile man," Hitler would commit suicide by the end of the month, as the Soviets closed in on his command post under the Chancellery. But several weeks before his death the Nazi leader ordered the Reichsbank's Dr. Funk to move more German gold and currency out of Berlin. The $300 million captured at the underground mine by no means represented all of Nazi Germany's financial resources.

On April 13, 1945, two trains loaded with bags of paper money left Berlin and headed south to Munich. The trains' progress was extremely slow because they had to avoid being detected by Allied warplanes.

Dr. Walther Funk, president of the Reichsbank. At the behest of Adolf Hitler, Funk moved gold and currency valued at hundreds of millions of dollars from the Reichsbank's headquarters in Berlin.

Finally, a bank official named Hans von Rosenberg-Lipinski, who was growing impatient with the delays, decided to take approximately 90 bags of currency from the trains and ship them directly to Munich by truck.

Meanwhile, a huge shipment of gold had also left Berlin, headed for Munich. But this was not the final destination of the Reichsbank's financial reserves. After the gold and currency arrived in Munich, they were taken outside the city to a mine for safekeeping. However, the mine, like so many other parts of Germany, had been damaged by an air raid, so the treasure was moved farther south to a town in the Bavarian Alps called Mittenwald. The Germans hoped that in this wooded, mountainous region the money might be safe from capture and could perhaps be used to rebuild the Nazi fortunes sometime in the future.

While part of the treasure was being moved to the Alps, more currency from Berlin arrived at the Munich branch of the Reichsbank. Here approximately $2 million was stolen by General Gottlob Berger, a high official in the Schutzstaffel, or SS, the dreaded Nazi security police. As German power collapsed, SS members hoped to use the money to help them escape and establish new lives for themselves after the war. Although General Berger was later captured, only part of the money he had stolen was recovered. The robbery of the Reichsbank had begun.

Meanwhile, in Berlin, the SS, led by Brigadier General Josef Spacil, had entered the main office of the Reichsbank, which had been relocated after the Allied bombing. In late April, Spacil and his men stole more than $9 million, including gold and jewels. The SS general flew out of Berlin to Salzburg, Austria, but he was later captured. However, most of what he had stolen was never recovered.

During the closing days of April, as Spacil was leaving Berlin, the treasure at Mittenwald was being unloaded. It included about $15 million in gold bars,

gold coins, and currency. The Reichsbank officials who accompanied the money to Mittenwald put it into the hands of Colonel Franz Wilhelm Pfeiffer. Colonel Pfeiffer was a German hero, a veteran of the eastern front, where the Nazis had been battling the Soviet armies since 1941. After enduring the fierce fighting and brutal winters on the Russian front, Pfeiffer had been rewarded with much easier duty at Mittenwald, where he ran an infantry training school.

By the time the Reichsbank treasure arrived, American armies were already approaching the area. Although Pfeiffer had some troops under his command, they couldn't hope to defend Mittenwald or preserve the Nazi gold. So the colonel and his officers came up

U.S. Third Army officers and an official of the Reichsbank examine the contents of an underground mine where the Nazis had concealed gold and currency valued at approximately $300 million.

with a plan: they would move the money deep into the Alpine woods and bury the treasure so the Americans would never find it.

The gold and currency were moved out of Mittenwald to a place called Forest House on the shores of Lake Walchen. Forest House belonged to Hans Neuhauser, the chief forester of the region, whose son—Hans Jr.—served with Pfeiffer. From here the heavy gold bars were moved by sturdy pack mules to one area of the woods. Pfeiffer's men dug holes and buried the treasure, then covered over the hiding place to disguise it. The currency was taken to another site, even deeper in the mountains, where Pfeiffer's men repeated the procedure.

They had buried the entire treasure by April 28, 1945—about the same time Berlin was falling to Soviet troops. Soon after the Red Army took control of the German capital, a high-ranking officer in Soviet intelligence went to the new headquarters of the Reichsbank, where he found approximately $400 million the Nazis hadn't evacuated from Berlin. This money became the property of the Soviet victors, who reasoned that they were entitled to get back some of what the war had cost them. It was another part of the giant haul taken from the German Reichsbank.

Outside Mittenwald, $15 million in Nazi treasure still lay buried in the woods, under the watchful eye of Colonel Pfeiffer. As the Americans approached the area, Pfeiffer cautioned his officers not to let anyone know where the money was hidden. If questioned, they were to say that SS troops had carried it off—a story that, he hoped, would be believable; the SS had already looted money throughout defeated Germany. However, American intelligence officers were not so easily deceived. Following the end of the war, American, British, and French armies occupied the western part of Germany. American intelligence had captured Reichsbank records from some of the branches located in the

German workers box up gold bars at the Reichsbank headquarters in Frankfurt. Though the Allies shipped recovered German currency and gold to Frankfurt, much of the treasure disappeared en route and was presumably stolen.

western sector. They knew that a large shipment of money had reached Mittenwald, and it would not be long before they found Colonel Pfeiffer.

Led by Lieutenant Herbert G. DuBois, an American squad of gold hunters arrived at Forest House and began questioning the men who had been involved in burying the treasure. But the Germans stuck by the story that the SS had removed the money, and no one admitted knowing where the treasure had been taken. For a time, the trail seemed to grow cold. DuBois could not find the money, or the SS, or Colonel Pfeiffer.

Pfeiffer, however, was beginning to grow worried

that someone might eventually tip off the Americans. With the help of some of his men, he returned to where the currency had been stashed and dug up part of it. Pfeiffer had decided to move some of the currency—which was much easier to carry than the heavy gold bars—to various farms in the Mittenwald area and bury small amounts in each location. He also took some of the money to a house where he was staying in nearby Garmisch-Partenkirchen. The house was owned by Luder von Blucher—one of Pfeiffer's officers—and his brother Hubert. More than $400,000 was buried in the ground outside the house.

Although Pfeiffer seemed to stay one step ahead of them, the Americans had not stopped looking for him or the money. U.S. officials arrested Hans Neuhauser, the chief forester, as well as some of Colonel Pfeiffer's officers, and they also rounded up some Reichsbank officials. In early June, one of these officers—Captain Heinz Ruger—finally broke under questioning and told the Americans where some of the gold was hidden. He took them to the area where the Germans had buried more than 350 bags, each containing two gold bars. This stash was valued at about $10 million. All the bags were recovered and sent to Munich for eventual shipment to the Foreign Exchange Depository in Frankfurt, Germany, where recovered German funds were being stored.

However, this wasn't all the gold that had been buried in the mountains near Mittenwald. A short time later, American officials recovered another cache of Nazi gold after a captured German officer gave them a tip to its whereabouts. This treasure was loaded on trucks and also sent to Frankfurt. But the gold never arrived—it simply disappeared and may have been stolen.

By June, Colonel Pfeiffer had grown tired of hiding from the Americans and decided to turn himself in. Hoping to avoid imprisonment by cooperating with the

American authorities, he confessed his role in hiding the currency, then digging up some of it and hiding it again in new locations. He revealed where most—but not all—of the currency had been hidden, and the American authorities dug it up and recovered several million dollars' worth. This money was turned in to the military government at Garmisch-Partenkirchen to be sent on to Frankfurt. But once again, the currency vanished, like much of the other Nazi gold.

However, some parts of the treasure were recovered. In late June, Captain Hans Neuhauser Jr.—one of Colonel Pfeiffer's officers, and the son of the chief forester—surrendered to the American army. He, too, hoped to avoid prison in return for revealing where he and some of Pfeiffer's other men had buried boxes of gold coins—part of the original shipment that had come to Mittenwald. This gold, worth about $800,000, was recovered after Neuhauser told the Americans where it was hidden.

Holding on to his trump card, Pfeiffer had still not revealed anything about the currency hidden in the garden outside the home of Hubert and Luder von Blucher, his friends in Garmisch-Partenkirchen. When he and some of his officers were threatened with jail terms, however, the German colonel finally came clean. The money buried in the garden was recovered and handed over to the U.S. Third Army. But once again, the currency disappeared on its way to Frankfurt and was probably stolen.

Pfeiffer eventually left Germany and moved to Argentina, like many other former Nazis. The missing Nazi treasure—more than $400 million—was never returned to the German government. Much of it was kept by the victorious Soviet Union; part may have been spent by private individuals to establish lavish lifestyles for themselves after the war. And some of the money may still be hidden in the area around Mittenwald.

THE BRINK'S JOB

By any measure, the Brink's holdup of 1950 must be considered a great robbery. Ingeniously conceived, meticulously planned, and boldly executed, the heist netted a huge payout for its participants. Indeed, the FBI called it "the perfect crime."

The Brink's job was masterminded by a small-time hoodlum named Anthony "Tony" Pino. Born on the island of Sicily in 1907, Pino came to America with his family when he was still a child. His father could find only menial work driving a delivery cart, and Tony's family lived in a dark, drafty tenement building in a poor section of Boston. Soon Tony was stealing coal from a nearby railroad yard for the stove that heated his family's cold apartment. By the age of seven, he had already joined a youth gang that specialized in shoplifting items from local merchants. Eventually, Tony's escapades would land him in court and earn him a sentence to reform school at age 15.

A Brink's armored truck. Directly attacking these vehicles, with their thick armor plating and bullet-proof glass, would require a small army. Tony Pino found an easier way: he obtained copies of the keys and followed the trucks around until they were left unattended.

As he grew older, Pino graduated to more-serious crimes. He became an expert safecracker and worked with a small gang of thieves to pull off a series of small robberies. Among his associates were Thomas "Sandy" Richardson, who had also begun his criminal career as a member of a youth gang, and James "Jimma" Faherty, a young man who worked part-time on the Boston docks. A fourth member of the team, considered very handy with a gun, was Michael Vincent Geagan. While still a teenager, Geagan had done time for armed robbery. In 1934, Geagan and Richardson stuck up city hall in Brockton, Massachusetts, getting away with more than $10,000 from the treasurer's department. Geagan was later arrested for the holdup and went to prison in 1935. Soon afterward Richardson, Faherty, and Pino were arrested and sentenced to prison for armed robbery. All of these men would eventually collaborate in the holdup of Brink's.

As a condition of his release from prison in 1944, Pino was expected to find a legitimate job. He went to work loading trucks on the night shift at Stop and Shop, a large food market. But his years behind bars had done nothing to dampen his interest in making money a much easier way—by committing robberies. Pino went back to shoplifting, then joined his old partner Sandy Richardson in robbing a lingerie factory. The two crooks silently entered the factory at night, and after Pino cracked the safe, they made off with more than $3,000. Richardson and Pino pulled off another successful robbery at a textile company with the help of a third hoodlum named John Adolph "Jazz" Maffie. Maffie generally made his living as a bookie, although he also dabbled in armed robbery.

Although these robberies provided Pino with some money, he dreamed of pulling off a multimillion-dollar heist. The opportunity he had been waiting for suddenly presented itself early one morning in 1944. As Pino walked along the dark Boston streets after finishing his night shift at Stop and Shop, he passed near the office of Brink's Incorporated. Founded in Chicago just before the Civil War, Brink's had begun as a transportation company but gradually came to specialize in delivering payrolls. In the early-morning darkness, the Brink's guards were loading a payroll for delivery to a factory in the Boston area. The payroll would be carried in a heavy Brink's armored truck (which was protected with bulletproof glass and steel armor), delivered to its destination, then distributed in pay envelopes to the workers at the factory.

His criminal interest piqued, Pino returned night after night to observe the procedures at the Brink's offices. Guards loaded sacks of money on armored trucks destined for many businesses in the greater Boston area. Pino invited Richardson to observe the

Brink's operation with him, and the two crooks realized there was a huge opportunity to pull off a major robbery—if they could just figure out how and when to strike. The armored trucks themselves were so well protected that it would take a small army to overpower them. Perhaps the thieves could strike while a truck was being loaded in front of the Brink's office, when a well-armed group of determined robbers might be able to overcome the guards. Or perhaps the gang could strike a plant after a payroll had been delivered.

Pino began following Brink's trucks to their destinations. He tailed one truck to the General Electric plant in Lynn, Massachusetts, near Boston. By talking to several GE employees, he learned that more than 25,000 people worked at the plant, and he estimated that the total payroll was approximately $2.5 million. But the paymaster's office at the plant was so well guarded that Pino and his men couldn't hope to make a successful robbery there. They would have to steal the payroll at the Brink's offices.

As he continued his surveillance of the Brink's operations, Pino saw one of the armored trucks enter a garage. To his delight, he had stumbled on the place where the company housed all of its vehicles. The huge garage wasn't heavily guarded, and Pino figured out a way to sneak in and look around. Inside, among the rows of parked armored cars and trucks, Pino made the most important discovery of his long criminal career— the keys to all the Brink's vehicles.

Accompanied by Sandy Richardson, Pino continued following Brink's armored trucks on the streets. One day, after dropping off a payroll at a factory, a truck stopped and the guards left it unattended while they went into a nearby coffee shop. Pino realized that he had plenty of time to sneak up behind the truck, unlock it with a duplicate of the key, and quickly pull out a few bags of money that were destined for another delivery.

The crooks used the same modus operandi with

other trucks in the fleet. Pino would often disguise himself as a Brink's worker so passersby wouldn't notice him as he walked up to the armored truck and quickly removed the money. Using this approach, the thieves stole an estimated $400,000. Amazingly, Brink's did nothing to prevent these thefts, such as increasing the number of guards on each truck, changing their routes, or ordering that the trucks never be left unattended.

But Pino and Richardson were not content simply to pilfer from the armored trucks. Together with other members of their gang, they began robbing some of the businesses where Brink's had made deliveries. On October 30, 1947, for example, they broke into a factory in Hyde Park, Massachusetts, wearing Halloween masks. The armed thieves headed for the vault room, where clerks were filling pay envelopes for the factory workers. Ordering the clerks to stop what they were doing and face the wall, the bandits stole more than $100,000 and made a clean getaway. A day later Pino's gang struck again at another company in south Boston only a few minutes after a Brink's truck had made its delivery.

The two holdups brought huge headlines in the press, which called them "the Halloween robberies." Since the gang members had long records as thieves, the police suspected they might be involved in the crimes. Geagan, Richardson, Faherty, and Pino were all brought in and questioned, but because there was no evidence to hold them, they were released.

The string of thefts had netted Pino and his colleagues a considerable amount of money, and the police couldn't link the bandits to any of the crimes. Still, the hoodlum who had spent almost his entire life breaking the law never considered quitting while he was ahead. He still dreamed of the monumental job that would cap his criminal career and make him a wealthy man: the theft of the General Electric payroll, worth more than $2.5 million. In 1948, Pino began carefully planning a robbery at the Brink's offices in Boston. After thorough observation of the pickup procedure, he devised a plan to overcome the guards and steal the money. The thieves intended to strike early in January 1949. Before the heist could occur, however, Brink's unexpectedly closed its offices and moved to a new location. Pino had no idea where that location was, and until he found it, the robbery would have to be postponed.

Pino began following Brink's trucks, and eventually one of them led him to the company's new location. Despite the recent robberies it had suffered at the hands of Pino's gang, Brink's security measures remained remarkably lax. From an observation post near the building, Pino found that he could easily look through the windows and watch Brink's employees at work. First they took the money out of the company's huge vault, then they counted it out to make up the payrolls. One evening, after all the employees had gone home, a door to the building was left open, and Pino sneaked inside. He discovered that the door locks to the building could easily be picked, so he went back repeatedly and roamed through the company offices, looking for alarms and hidden cameras that might be used to detect a robbery and alert the police. Although Brink's had taken some precautions, Pino found that the vault room would be easy to enter without tripping any detection system.

Breaking into the vault itself would be another matter. Its walls were made of thick concrete, and the door was built of sturdy steel. Cutting through the door with a blowtorch would take hours, and the thieves would likely be discovered during the robbery. Pino eventually realized that the gang would need to strike the vault when it was already open. By observing the Brink's operations during 1949, he discovered that the vault employees usually stayed behind and finished their work after the rest of the staff had left for the evening.

Pino's plan called for the gang to approach the

Joseph O'Keefe, a partici-
pant in the Brink's robbery,
in custody for a different
crime, 1954. Sentenced to
a prison term, O'Keefe
appealed to Brink's job colleagues to aid his family
while he remained behind
bars. Their refusal to answer
this call for help ultimately
ruined the perfect crime.

Brink's offices near closing time, when it would already
be dark and their movements would be harder to see.
One of the crooks would be stationed at an observation
post with a full view of the company's windows. He
would make sure that the vault was still open as the
gang approached the building. Pino feared that if the
vault was closed, even if the crooks reached the vault
room and surprised the Brink's employees, the clerks
might not reveal the combination to the vault.

On the first attempt to pull off the robbery, the
thieves approached the building. But at the last

minute, they had to turn back because a signal from the lookout told them that the vault had been closed.

The robbers tried again on Tuesday, January 17, 1950. Pino knew from a schedule of deliveries he had observed in the Brink's offices that there would be less money in the vault on Tuesday night. But repeated observations had revealed that the vault was closed between 7:00 and 7:15 every Tuesday, so the gang should be able to time their entry almost to the minute. That evening the crooks assembled near the Brink's building wearing heavy jackets, caps, and masks to conceal their identities. Pino stayed in the getaway truck as Richardson, Faherty, Geagan, Maffie, and several other crooks prepared to enter the building, which was quiet because most of the employees had already gone home. A signal from the lookout indicated that the vault was still open, so the robbery proceeded.

The men entered the building and headed toward the vault room. Pointing his gun at the clerks, one of the crooks demanded, "Okay, boys, put them in the air." The startled clerks complied, raising their hands. But a locked metal grille separated the thieves from the Brink's employees in the vault. When the masked robbers ordered that the grille be opened, there was some hesitation. Eventually, however, one of the employees did as he was told, deciding that the thieves might start shooting if they encountered any resistance.

The robbers forced the Brink's staff to the floor, tied their hands behind them, and taped their mouths. Then they entered the open vault and started putting money into sacks. In a few minutes, they had finished their criminal work. Leaving the building as easily as they had entered, they jumped into the waiting truck and made their escape, having stolen almost $2.8 million—the largest robbery in the United States up to that time.

But it wasn't long before a Brink's employee managed to wriggle free of his bonds and sound the alarm.

A short time later, sirens were wailing as Boston police converged on the Brink's building. Once they realized what had happened, the police set up roadblocks on all roads leading out of the city; they also began watching the airports and bus terminals for any suspicious characters who might be trying to leave with heavy satchels, presumably filled with cash.

However, Pino and his confederates had no intention of leaving Boston. They already had a hiding place to stash the money. And shortly after the crime, they had disposed of their disguises and were seen at their favorite restaurants or bars by eyewitnesses who would provide convincing alibis.

Eight men charged in the Brink's robbery await the beginning of their trial, August 7, 1956. From left: James Faherty, Michael Geagan, Sandy Richardson, Joseph McGinnis, Tony Pino, Vincent Costa, Jazz Maffie, and Henry Baker.

The robbery drew the immediate attention of the Federal Bureau of Investigation, which assigned the case a high priority because of the huge amount of money involved. FBI agents repeatedly interviewed the Brink's vault room employees and questioned informants from Boston's criminal underworld. Suspecting Pino's gang, the agents put the men under surveillance, but no concrete evidence ever emerged. The masks and clothes the thieves had worn during the robbery were never found, the thieves hadn't left any fingerprints at the scene of the crime, and none of the money had been recovered.

Under federal law, charges for armed robbery had to be filed within three years of the commission of the crime. Once this period—called the statute of limitations—had expired, the crime couldn't be prosecuted in federal court, even if indisputable proof of the perpetrators' guilt later surfaced. At the end of three years, however, the FBI hadn't come close to making a case. Pino had done such an impeccable job planning the robbery that there was no incriminating evidence to link his gang to the theft. It looked like the perfect crime.

But in Massachusetts the statute of limitations for armed robbery was six years, not three, so state police took over the case. As the months and years passed with no good leads, however, it seemed that the crime would remain unsolved.

Meanwhile, one of the thieves, Joseph O'Keefe, was sentenced to prison for committing another robbery. While O'Keefe was behind bars, he wrote to his Brink's job colleagues and asked them to help his family, which was in desperate financial straits. None of the crooks answered this call to help—and it would cost them dearly. With only 11 days remaining on the statute of limitations in Massachusetts, O'Keefe decided to tell the police everything he knew about the great Brink's robbery.

Pino and the other robbers were rounded up and put on trial in August 1956. With O'Keefe's testimony against them, they were found guilty and sentenced to life in prison. Greed and dishonor among thieves had ruined the perfect crime.

THE GREAT
TRAIN ROBBERY

T he newspapers called it "history's greatest robbery" and compared the thieves to the Jesse James gang. In 1963, about a dozen robbers stopped the Up Special, a mail train, as it sped along the tracks at 70 miles per hour from Glasgow, Scotland, toward its destination in London. The daring heist netted over $7 million—far more than the James brothers had ever even dreamed of stealing.

What came to be known as "the great train robbery" was the brainchild of several members of England's criminal underworld. One of them was Buster Edwards, a thief in his early thirties who also owned a London club. Edwards and an accomplice named Gordon Goody led a small gang of thieves who held up local bookies. In 1961, determined to try something bigger,

An English policeman stands guard over the mail coach from which thieves stole £2,552,000, or more than $7 million, in 1963's "great train robbery."

Reunion: The masterminds of the great train robbery, on tour to promote a book about their caper, 1979. From left: Roger Cordrey, Bruce Reynolds, Buster Edwards.

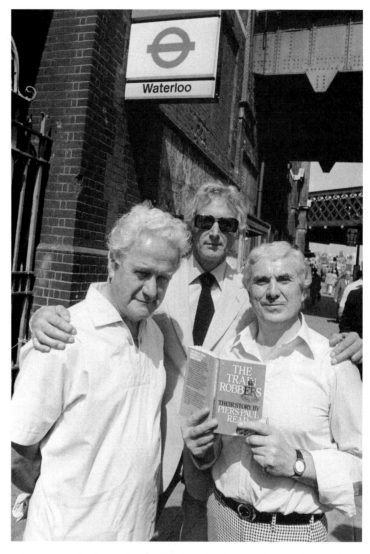

they traveled to Cork, Ireland, where they planned to rob a large bank. But before they could pull off the robbery, the police discovered the plan, and the two thieves were lucky to escape without being arrested.

A year later, Goody and Edwards were joined by an experienced crook named Charlie Wilson, who ran a grocery business when he was not committing robberies. Together the three men held up the central office of a large railroad. Waiting until after the payroll for the railroad workers had been delivered by armored car, they broke in, overpowered the clerks in the office, and made off with more than $70,000.

A short time later, Goody, Wilson, and Edwards were involved in an even more daring robbery. In 1962, they held up the headquarters of a large British airline. This time one of their accomplices was Bruce Reynolds. A tall, dark-haired man with glasses, Reynolds had earned a reputation for planning successful crimes. Dressed as respectable businessmen, the thieves entered the building in broad daylight, then went to the top floor and waited until an armored delivery truck had brought in the money. Next the men quickly descended in the elevator and, donning stocking masks, demanded all the money from the terrified airline staff before it could be safely locked away. Escaping with almost $175,000, the thieves sped away in shiny Jaguars—one of them driven by Reynolds's good friend Roy James. The spectacular robbery made headlines throughout England, and the clues eventually led police to the doorsteps of the gang members. Goody and Wilson were put on trial, but because they had worn masks, no one at the scene of the crime could actually identify them. This fact, plus excellent work by their lawyer, a man named Brian Field, helped them win acquittal. All of these men—Field, Goody, Wilson, Reynolds, James, and Edwards—would play key roles in the great train robbery.

Meanwhile, another man who would become a member of the gang had already begun robbing trains. Roger Cordrey ran a legitimate flower shop, but he also liked gambling and constantly needed extra money to pay off his losses. Cordrey began with small thefts. He would take his seat on a local train, and while the conductor was busy in another area, he would go to the mail car and break into it. Then he would head for the specially marked high-value packages. These were packages that contained money. With the help of an associate named Frank Munroe, Cordrey would steal what he could, conceal the cash, and leave the train before anyone caught him.

Eventually, Cordrey began to plan much larger robberies, and he soon focused on the signals along the railroad tracks. Like traffic lights on a roadway, the train signals regulated the flow of train traffic. If a light was green, an engineer knew his train could continue traveling at full speed; if the signal was yellow, he had to slow down the train because the next signal might be red, which required him to bring the train to a full stop. Cordrey figured out how to cover up a green light using a cloth and illuminate the yellow one, slowing down a train. Then he turned on the red light farther down the track, bringing the train to a stop. Once it had halted, Cordrey would break into a mail car and steal all the high-value packages. Of course, he couldn't do all these things alone. He worked with a gang of thieves that included Munroe and two experienced crooks named Tom Wisbey and Bob Welch. Once the thieves had robbed the mail car, they quickly escaped with the money before the railroad authorities realized that the train had been stopped improperly.

Bruce Reynolds and Buster Edwards had also begun robbing trains, but they lacked Cordrey's know-how about changing the signals. Therefore, their capers weren't as profitable. In 1963, however, they learned about an unusual opportunity to intercept the Up Special as it traveled south from Glasgow to London. Although the mail train had been running for more than a century, it had never been robbed. While it hurtled south during the night, picking up mail from stations along the way, more than 70 postal employees aboard the cars sorted the letters and packages so they would be ready for delivery the next day. The second car behind the engine was a special high-value coach, which carried money. During August, Great Britain had a three-day weekend, called a bank holiday, and vacationers often traveled north into Scotland to enjoy a few days off. After the holiday was over, the Scottish banks returned the English currency to London in exchange for Scottish currency held by England. The English money was transported from Scotland in the high-value coach of the Up Special.

Reynolds and Edwards realized that they could rob the Up Special only if they could somehow stop the train in a remote area where no one would see them. That's where Cordrey came in: he knew how to manipulate the train signals. The three men decided to pool their resources and bring their gangs together to pull off the robbery. But it would not be easy. First, they had to find a location that fit their requirements—an isolated spot away from a major railroad station with two signals that Cordrey could control. Eventually, they found just the right place near Leighton Buzzard, a town in Bedfordshire, north of London. For weeks before the robbery, the men scouted the area. They examined the signal lights, and Cordrey made sure he could manipulate them successfully.

Once the train had been stopped, the men planned to uncouple the engine and the two cars behind it—one of which was the high-value coach. They learned how to uncouple train cars and found an engineer who would operate the engine with its two coaches, pulling them away from the rest of the train. They planned to take the train down the track to nearby Bridego Bridge, where getaway vehicles would be parked. Then the robbers would break into the high-value coach, unload the bags of money, put them in their vehicles, and make their escape. All of this would occur in the middle of the night, while the surrounding countryside was asleep.

Since Reynolds and Edwards were convinced that they wouldn't have enough time to leave Leighton Buzzard and reach a major highway before their crime was discovered, they looked for a location nearby to remain undercover for a few days until they could

The thieves administered a beating to Up Special engineer Jack Mills—but then realized they needed him to move the engine and high-value coach.

escape unnoticed. Through a local real estate agent, the thieves located a farm that was up for sale. Called Leatherslade Farm, it stood atop a hill and would give the gang a view of the surrounding area, yet it was hidden from nosy neighbors by a large stand of trees. Leatherslade was approximately 25 miles from Bridego Bridge, where the robbery would occur. To keep their identities hidden, the thieves took the precaution of purchasing the farm through Brian Field, the lawyer, and John Wheater, who ran the law firm for which Field worked.

A few days before the robbery, Reynolds, Edwards, Cordrey, and the other men moved into Leatherslade Farm. They had stocked the farmhouse with food and brought three vehicles to transport them to and from Leighton Buzzard. The men planned to wear woolen caps with eyeholes over their heads to prevent anyone from identifying them. As the day of the robbery arrived, they went over the plans carefully and rehearsed all the steps one last time.

Just after midnight on August 8, 1963, a truck and two Land Rovers pulled away from Leatherslade Farm and headed for Bridego Bridge. The robbers parked their vehicles nearby, then snipped the telephone wires to cut off all communications from the area. Roger Cordrey and John Daly, another member of the gang, took their positions—one at each signal light—while Bruce Reynolds waited up ahead with a walkie-talkie, ready to radio a signal when the train was approaching. As the night wore on, the Up Special headed south toward Leighton Buzzard carrying 12 coaches packed with mail. Second from the engine was the high-value coach, filled with more than 125 bags containing paper money. The diesel engine itself was driven by Jack Mills, a veteran engineer, assisted by a young fireman named David Whitby. It was three o'clock before the train began to approach the first signal. Reynolds put the walkie-talkie up to his mouth: "It's coming down, chaps," he said. "This is the real thing."

Mills spotted the signal up ahead beside the tracks. It had turned yellow, so he began to slow the train. As he moved the Up Special 1,000 yards down the track, he could see the next signal, which hung high overhead above the train line. It was glowing red in the darkness, and Mills brought the engine to a halt. He asked Whitby to leave the train, go to the telephone that was next to the signal, and call ahead to find out what was causing the delay. As Whitby reached the telephone, he noticed that the lines had been cut. Something was wrong. Whitby looked back toward the train and saw a figure in the darkness next to one of the coaches. He walked over, thinking a postal employee had left the train. But as he approached, he realized that the man was wearing a mask. It was Buster Edwards, and before Whitby could turn and run away, Edwards had grabbed him. With the help of two accomplices, Edwards dragged the young fireman toward the engine. The thieves entered the cab, overpowered Mills, and quickly took control of the train.

Meanwhile, other members of the gang had uncoupled the engine and first two cars from the rest of the Up Special. Everything was going according to plan. Then an unforeseen problem occurred. Unfortunately for the thieves, the engineer they had brought with them didn't know how to operate the type of diesel engine that was pulling the Up Special. Mills, who had been beaten over the head and handcuffed, was dragged forward and ordered to move the train toward Bridego Bridge.

Once the train had come to a halt there, the thieves used crowbars to break through the windows and door into the high-value car. The startled postal workers were forced to stand aside while the gang carried out 120 bags of currency. After loading the bags into the truck, the thieves ordered the mail employees to lie on the floor along with the engineer and the fireman. "Now don't move for half an hour or we'll be back," one of the bandits said in a threatening voice. They left the train and drove away into the night—the entire robbery having taken only about half an hour.

Dawn was breaking as the men returned to Leatherslade Farm. In the meantime, the mail workers on the train had realized that the robbers were not returning. The engineer and the fireman hailed a passing train and rode to a nearby town, where they telephoned the local police. Led by Detective Superintendent Malcolm Fewtrell, an investigation began less than two hours

Aerial view of Leatherslade Farm, the train robbers' hideout, after the police raid. Fingerprints the thieves left in the house would lead to arrests.

after the robbery had been committed. Taking no chances that the thieves might escape, Fewtrell's men called in the Metropolitan Police at Scotland Yard, whose forensic experts could help solve the case.

Although the thieves had planned to hide out at the farm for a few days, radio news broadcasts soon after the robbery carried descriptions of their vehicles, which had apparently been observed by locals. In addition, news reports revealed that the police believed the robbers were still in the area, because there hadn't been enough time for them to reach the main highways and escape without being seen. Hearing these news bulletins, the bandits realized that they had to move fast to avoid being tracked down at the farmhouse. After dividing up the loot, they quickly loaded it into some new vehicles and left everything else behind. They had expected an accomplice, called the Dustman, to come in and clean up the farmhouse, removing any fingerprints or other evidence that might link the gang members to the crime. Much to the dismay of Reynolds and Edwards, however, the Dustman hadn't shown up to do his job.

By the time the robbers beat their hasty retreat, the police were already closing in on the farmhouse. Eyewitnesses had reported seeing suspicious-looking men at Leatherslade Farm. When a neighbor dropped by to talk to them, they claimed to be housepainters who had been hired to spruce up the place. On August 12, four days after the robbery, the police raided the farmhouse. They found uneaten food, abandoned mail bags, clothing worn by the thieves, and even a small amount of money that had been left behind. More important, they found fingerprints. Although the thieves were always supposed to wear gloves throughout their stay at Leatherslade, they had gotten careless from time to time, assuming that the Dustman would see to it that any prints were removed.

From the fingerprints police identified a number of the robbers, including Roy James, John Daly, Tom

Wisbey, Charlie Wilson, and Bruce Reynolds. Most of them were soon arrested. However, Reynolds and another leader of the robbery, Buster Edwards, escaped from England and would not be captured until several years later.

Roger Cordrey had taken his share of the loot and headed south to Bournemouth, a seaside resort in southern England. Accompanying him was an old friend, William Boal. Cordrey and Boal hoped to stash the money until the publicity surrounding the train robbery had died down. Once they reached Bournemouth, Boal tried to rent a garage. When he paid the owner by peeling off several bills from a large roll of money, she became suspicious and called the police. The police promptly arrested Boal and Cordrey, who led them to about $400,000 from the holdup. Police also arrested the lawyers Brian Field and John Wheater, who had purchased Leatherslade Farm for the robbers.

More of the money was recovered in mid-August when two people riding a motorcycle to work stopped to take a break near some woods. There they found a bag and a briefcase filled with money, and called the police. The money totaled more than $300,000. The rest of the loot from the heist, however, was never found. The thieves probably spent at least some of it.

Most of the criminals involved in the great train robbery were finally brought to trial in January 1964. Although none of the postal workers could identify the robbers, fingerprint evidence tied most of the gang to the crime. The jurors also heard the testimony of Jack Mills, who had been beaten over the head by the thieves, and of his assistant, David Whitby. After deliberating for two days, the jury found all the men guilty. The judge meted out stiff sentences—from 24 to 30 years in prison. Wheater received only three years because it seemed clear that he had not been directly involved in the robbery.

350 Pounds of Cash

On April 22, 1981, environmentalists in the United States and around the world marked Earth Day, an annual observance designed to spotlight the condition of the world's environment. In Tucson, Arizona, three men with a different sort of "green" agenda marked the occasion in their own way: they held up the First National Bank of Arizona depository, a central banking facility that distributed cash to branch offices. The thieves stole more than $3 million, making it the largest bank robbery in U.S. history.

The daring and lucrative robbery at the Tucson bank depository was the brainchild of David Lee Grandstaff, a 38-year-old career criminal. One of six children, Grandstaff had grown up in a poor section of Des Moines, Iowa. Although both of his parents worked, they barely earned enough to support their

Tucson, Arizona, was the site of a 1981 bank robbery that netted a record $3.3 million.

family. As a child, Grandstaff began stealing ice cream from local stores and taking groceries for his siblings. Early in his life, he developed a deep-seated anger and resentment toward people who had more money than his family. Indeed, Grandstaff was arrested for breaking into the homes of well-off residents of Des Moines and wrecking their furniture. He was lucky that a judge opted not to send him to reform school for the crime.

Unfortunately, his narrow escape from reform school didn't deter David Grandstaff from committing further crimes. After illegally entering the basement of a Coca-Cola plant, he stole the keys to the company's soft-drink vending machines in the Des Moines area and began robbing them. He and an accomplice named George Weir also began stealing bicycles. Although they were eventually caught, both boys received probation.

A few months later, however, Grandstaff was arrested for stealing an automobile. This time he was sent to reform school, his first sentence behind bars. But soon after his release, he was picked up for another crime and sent back again. Finally, at the age of 17, Grandstaff found himself doing time, for armed robbery, in the Iowa state prison at Fort Madison. He had finally joined the hardened criminals.

Prison life was extremely harsh, but it didn't convince David Grandstaff to go straight so he would never be placed behind bars again. In 1966, he and Weir picked up where they had left off. Grandstaff had taken a job at a gasoline station as part of his parole from prison, and the two friends decided to hold up that station. With guns drawn, they forced the attendants to hand over more than $3,000, then made a successful escape.

Grandstaff followed the gas station robbery with a series of holdups at grocery stores. He carefully studied each location, noting when armored trucks arrived with shipments of cash. Shortly after an armored truck had

Over the course of his long criminal career, David Lee Grandstaff was involved in robberies totaling millions of dollars.

left, Grandstaff would march into the store with Weir and another accomplice, Mike See, and rob the store at gunpoint. Although the local police had their suspicions, they could never pin anything on Grandstaff and his companions, and the thieves were never caught.

Grocery stores, however, didn't seem quite lucrative enough for Grandstaff and his friends. On Valentine's Day in 1967, the three bandits decided to hit the First National Bank in Kellogg, Iowa. Instead of walking into the bank in broad daylight, however, Grandstaff had devised a more subtle plan. He found out where the bank's president, Raymond Welle, and his wife lived. While Welle was at work, Grandstaff and his accomplices entered the president's home and took his wife hostage. When the bank president arrived home that night, he discovered, to his shock, that three armed, masked bandits were holding his wife. The bandits threatened to harm Mrs. Welle unless her husband helped them rob the First National Bank. He complied. While his two accomplices waited with the bank president's wife, Grandstaff accompanied Welle to the bank. Welle opened the vault, and Grandstaff removed $15,000.

The daring robbery immediately attracted the attention of the FBI, which suspected that it might have been committed by the same men who were involved in the grocery store thefts. Agents began a surveillance of one of Weir's friends, who decided to cooperate with the authorities. When Weir contacted the FBI informant, agents arrested him. Soon afterward, Grandstaff, realizing that he would be implicated in the holdup, decided to give himself up. In 1967, he was sent to the maximum-security federal penitentiary at Leavenworth, Kansas. He would remain behind bars for the next eight years.

After his release in 1975, Grandstaff returned to his home in Des Moines. Although he had earned a college degree while at Leavenworth, Grandstaff had almost never made a living at any occupation besides robbery, so he went back to what he knew best. Once again, he began staking out supermarkets and noting the delivery schedules of armored trucks. Meanwhile, George Weir had joined a car thief named Douglas Bruce Fenimore in several bank holdups. Grandstaff asked Fenimore to help him rob the same Coca-Cola plant where he had stolen the vending machine keys as a child. It was a carefully planned job. Grandstaff and an accomplice named Mike Gabriel entered the building just after an armored truck delivery. After taking the money, they jumped into a getaway car driven by Fenimore. The men could not be identified, nor did they leave any fingerprints, so there was no evidence to link them directly to the crime. The robbery netted the thieves $300,000.

Grandstaff moved out of Iowa and continued his criminal activities in other parts of the country where he wasn't known and would presumably create less suspicion among the authorities. He led a gang of thieves that included Gabriel, Fenimore, a gambler named Doug Brown, and several other men. In May 1980, they robbed a jewelry store in Phoenix. While part of the gang held the store clerks at gunpoint, the others quickly unloaded trays of expensive jewelry into their bags. The robbery was completed in a few minutes, and the men escaped with more than $1 million in precious jewels.

Fencing the jewelry, however, proved more difficult than stealing it. One of the thieves tried to sell the jewelry through a contact in Des Moines, who immediately called the FBI, and the thief was arrested. Soon the trail led to Grandstaff and Fenimore, who were also taken into custody. But neither of them planned to remain in Des Moines for very long. Out on bail while awaiting trial, Grandstaff and Fenimore, joined by Brown, fled.

After holding up a bank in Denver, the three men eventually returned to Arizona, where Grandstaff began looking for another place to rob. A large enough heist might enable him to retire from crime, at least temporarily. As he had in the past, Grandstaff began watching armored trucks to determine the best time to strike. Now his intended target was a bank. But he soon realized that an individual branch bank offered a small payoff compared with the central bank, where the armored trucks picked up money for delivery to the branches. Grandstaff decided to rob one such depository—that of the First National Bank of Arizona in Tucson—but only after he had carefully staked it out. By repeated observation, Grandstaff discovered that the manager and his assistant arrived each morning without fail about 20 minutes before the other bank employees and the armored trucks. He concluded that this 20 minutes would provide a sufficient window of opportunity to carry out a robbery.

On the morning of April 22, 1981, Grandstaff, Fenimore, and Brown pulled into the parking lot of the depository in a van. Shortly afterward, the manager, Bud Grainger, drove up to the depository, left his car, and unlocked the bank door. Before he had time to enter, the van was behind him and the crooks had jumped out and forced Grainger inside. Now the men waited for the assistant manager, David Harris, to arrive. Harris and Grainger had separate combinations, both of which were necessary to open the main vault. A few minutes later, Harris appeared at the front door and Grainger let him in. Once inside, the assistant manager was startled to find himself surrounded by gunmen.

The two bank employees opened the vault, then Grainger—after some hesitation—agreed to open the drawers that contained the cash. The thieves tied Harris and Grainger up, then feverishly stuffed money into sacks they had brought. In their haste they reportedly scattered about $500,000 in small bills on the floor of the vault. Despite this considerable waste, they managed to load their sacks with a whole lot of money—an estimated 350 pounds' worth. The total value of that currency was approximately $3.3 million.

The robbers finished just before eight o'clock, when the armored trucks were due to arrive, and rapidly drove the van out of the parking lot. A short distance away, they abandoned the van, quickly switched to other cars, and drove west.

After Harris and Grainger were freed, they immediately called the local police. Soon the FBI had also entered the investigation of the robbery, which agents suspected might have been the work of Grandstaff and his gang.

The three thieves, meanwhile, had reached south-

After the FBI arrested Douglas Bruce Fenimore (at left) in Des Moines, he agreed to testify against David Lee Grandstaff and Douglas Wayne Brown, his partners in the First National Bank heist. Unfortunately for the prosecution, the jury had serious doubts about Fenimore's credibility.

ern California, where they stopped at a motel to divide up the money. Then each man went his own way. Once again, there were no fingerprints or eyewitness identifications of the three men. The FBI agents had only their hunches to go on.

Agents began showing pictures of the three men around Tucson. A waitress at a restaurant where they had eaten identified Fenimore, but she was less sure about Grandstaff and Brown. Eventually the getaway car that Fenimore had used was discovered at an airport after the thief had left it there and taken a flight eastward. But the three men could not definitively be placed in Tucson at the same time, and no hard evidence tied them to the bank robbery. Plus, their current whereabouts were unknown.

Fenimore made the FBI's job a lot easier by foolishly returning to Des Moines to visit his girlfriend. He didn't know, of course, that the FBI had found an eyewitness to place him in Tucson and had also tied him to one of the getaway cars. The agents were certain he had participated in the robbery. In Des Moines, FBI agents surrounded Fenimore's car. But the robber refused to go quietly, crashing through the agents' cars and leading them on a high-speed chase before finally being captured.

Fearful of receiving a long prison term, Fenimore decided to cooperate with the authorities in return for the promise of a reduced sentence. He revealed everything he knew about the Tucson bank robbery—including the names of his two accomplices. With the information from Fenimore, the FBI intensified the search for Grandstaff and Brown. A tip from an informant finally led the agents to a hotel in Denver, where both men were arrested. But no money found in their possession at the time of their arrest could be traced back to the First National Bank cash depository.

Thus the case against Brown and Grandstaff rested mainly on the testimony of Fenimore. At first, however, Fenimore balked at agreeing to face his accomplices in court, so the FBI held them on charges arising from the Phoenix jewelry store robbery. But once Fenimore agreed to testify openly, the case against Brown and Grandstaff moved forward. Unfortunately for the prosecution, Fenimore didn't strike the jury as a particularly credible witness. The defense made it clear that he was testifying after making a deal for a reduced sentence. Grandstaff's lawyer also emphasized that Fenimore had lied many times in the past and was probably lying again about the First National Bank robbery.

Since no one but Fenimore seemed absolutely sure that Grandstaff and Brown had actually been in Tucson, and no physical evidence tied them to the robbery, the jury found them not guilty. Afterward, Grandstaff shared his story with a Tucson newspaper reporter—and because the Fifth Amendment to the U.S. Constitution prohibits the government from retrying defendants who have been acquitted of a crime on the same charges, there was nothing the authorities could now do to bring him to justice. He and Brown had gotten away with the biggest bank robbery in American history.

AMERICA'S BIGGEST ART HEIST

The impulse to create art is older than civilization itself. As long ago as 15,000 B.C., primitive humans adorned the walls of their caves with paintings.

In the modern world, art continues to attract countless museum goers inspired by its power to convey the emotion, beauty, and turmoil of the human experience. Among a considerably smaller group of people, the desire to *possess* art is also strong. Collectors will pay vast sums of money for a great piece of art, particularly when its creator is a famous artist. Paintings by Vincent van Gogh and Pablo Picasso, for example, have sold for more than $80 million each.

When a commodity is that valuable, some of society's more criminally oriented types will be tempted to steal it. So while many great robberies have involved stealing cash—which is, after all, easy to haul away and even easier to spend—some of the most famous heists in history have involved art. In 1990, a renowned

Courtyard of the Isabella Stewart Gardner Museum in Boston. In 1990, thieves disguised as police officers made off with a dozen of the art museum's masterpieces.

museum in Boston was the site of one such robbery, which has the distinction of being the greatest art heist in the annals of American crime. The thieves stole paintings worth an estimated $300 million, and 10 years later none of the art has yet been recovered.

During the early 20th century, the most prominent art patron in Boston was an elderly, stately-looking woman named Isabella Stewart Gardner. With a fortune inherited from her father and late husband, Mrs. Gardner created a large and impressive art collection. Assisted by the art connoisseur Bernard Berenson, she bought almost 300 paintings. These included magnificent works by Dutch masters such as Rembrandt and Jan Vermeer, French impressionist painters like Edgar Degas, and American artists like John Singer Sargent. To display her paintings, Mrs. Gardner designed an Italian-style palace with a beautiful inner courtyard that stretched upward to a glass ceiling. Art lovers flocked to her palazzo, not only to see the paintings but also to enjoy concerts by well-known singers and musicians. Mrs. Gardner lived on the top floor of the building until her death in 1924. According to her will, none of the paintings she had collected were ever to be removed from the museum.

Mrs. Gardner's will notwithstanding, some of the paintings were removed during the early-morning hours of March 18, 1990. Wearing false mustaches and police uniforms, two men knocked on a door of the Isabella Stewart Gardner Museum at 1:24 A.M. They convinced the two guards on duty that they were responding to a call about a disturbance on the museum grounds. After the guards opened the door—contrary to their regulations—the thieves quickly overpowered them and slapped on handcuffs. Forcing them into the basement of the museum, the intruders further restrained the guards with duct tape. Then they went upstairs and got to work.

Because of the peculiarities of the Gardner

Museum's alarm system, the thieves could afford to take their time. When an alarm at the museum was tripped, only the guard desk would be alerted; the guards could then press a button that would notify the police directly. But since the people who should have been at the guard desk were now tied up in the basement, the police weren't going to be notified. So over the next hour and a half, the robbers removed many of the museum's most valuable paintings—in some cases cutting them right out of their frames. The huge art haul included two paintings and an etching by Rembrandt, five canvases by Degas, and one each by Vermeer, the French painter Édouard Manet, and the Dutch artist Govaert Flinck. In addition, a 3,000-year-old bronze container from China's Shang Dynasty was taken. Before they left, the thieves removed the videotapes from the museum's surveillance cameras. By the time the guards freed themselves and called the police, the thieves were long gone.

It was an enormous loss for the Gardner Museum, which had no theft insurance to cover such a robbery. Even if it had, the paintings, as unique objects, would still be irreplaceable. Although the value of the stolen canvases was estimated at $300 million, the paintings were actually considered priceless.

Over the next several years, police and the FBI followed numerous leads, but each proved to be a dead end. The Gardner Museum offered a reward of $5 million for information leading to the return of the paintings, but no one came forward.

No one came forward, that is, until 1997. In that year a small-time crook named William Youngworth suddenly announced that he could lead authorities to the stolen art. Youngworth, an antiques dealer who had been in and out of prison, had recently been convicted of car theft. He offered to help recover the paintings in return for the $5 million reward and the promise that he would not be sentenced to prison for the car theft. In

Famous art thief Myles Connor Jr. (above) and his friend William P. Youngworth (opposite page) both claimed they could lead authorities to the stolen paintings—in exchange for the $5 million reward and their freedom. Ultimately, however, the two criminals couldn't or wouldn't produce the canvases.

addition, he wanted to secure the release of his friend Myles J. Connor Jr. Considered America's most famous art thief, Connor had been doing time behind bars since 1990 for trying to sell several stolen paintings. Before that, he had been involved in the theft of a Rembrandt from the Museum of Fine Arts in Boston as well as the robbery of several valuable paintings by famous American artists.

Although Connor had been in prison at the time of the Gardner heist, the FBI believed that he might have masterminded the robbery from his jail cell. Connor later claimed that the real culprits were two crooks named Bobby Donati and David Houghton. Both men died within two years of the robbery, with Donati probably the victim of a gangland slaying. While Connor admitted that he had once considered looting the Gardner Museum with Donati, he denied responsibility for the actual robbery.

Youngworth and Connor had spent time together in Walpole State Prison in Massachusetts. There the two men had become close friends, Youngworth said; now he wanted to do his friend a favor by securing his release. What Youngworth never explained, however, was how he had come into possession of the stolen paintings.

For his part, Connor told authorities that Donati and Houghton had informed him that in the event anything happened to them, they would leave him information regarding the whereabouts of the stolen paintings. But, Connor insisted, he had to be freed from prison to retrieve that information.

Meanwhile, a reporter for the *Boston Herald* named Tom Mashberg had begun investigating the Gardner heist. In mid-August 1997, he received a mysterious telephone call. The caller told Mashberg that he could see some of the stolen paintings if he went to a deserted location on the night of August 18. Mashberg agreed, and at the designated spot he was met by two men in two cars. Mashberg got into one of the cars and was driven to a warehouse, taken inside, and led up several flights of stairs. The man who accompanied him then unlocked the door to a room, removed something that had been rolled up inside a long tube, and showed it to Mashberg. It looked like the Rembrandt painting *Storm on the Sea of Galilee,* which had been stolen from the Gardner Museum. Mashberg was also given photographs of the other paintings that had been taken in the robbery, along with paint chips from the Rembrandt as further proof that it was genuine. One of

the men who had taken the reporter to the warehouse said that William Youngworth had sent them.

Shortly after Mashberg's nighttime journey, the *Boston Herald* ran a large headline stating: "WE'VE SEEN IT!" Mashberg was convinced that the Rembrandt he had seen was real and that the photographs he had been given showed the other paintings taken in the Gardner heist. The *Herald* hired an art expert to provide independent confirmation. He concluded that the paint chips were from the Rembrandt. Youngworth was apparently telling the truth.

But the FBI and officials of the Gardner Museum weren't so sure. They couldn't say whether the Rembrandt was genuine or simply a well-painted fake. The

Rembrandt's Storm on the Sea of Galilee. *Had investigative reporter Tom Mashberg been shown the real thing or a well-painted fake? Expert opinion was split.*

paint chips are "not what they purport to be," a statement from the museum announced.

William Youngworth's later actions seemed to justify the museum's skepticism. When authorities asked him to produce any of the paintings stolen in the robbery, Youngworth wouldn't or couldn't do it. Perhaps the hoodlum had no direct involvement in or knowledge of the robbery and might simply have been trying to con the Gardner Museum and law enforcement authorities. Whatever the case, Youngworth was sentenced to a prison term for the auto theft, while his friend, the art thief Myles Connor Jr., remained behind bars.

Who actually stole the paintings from the Gardner Museum? A decade after the crime, only the thieves know for certain. The canvases may be in the possession of a private collector—in the United States or abroad— or they may still be stashed somewhere while the robbers decide what to do with them. The Rembrandts, the Vermeer, the Manet, and the works by Degas taken in the Gardner heist remain among an estimated 100,000 stolen paintings, with a total value of approximately $6 billion, that have never been recovered.

Myles Connor Jr. once declared, "There isn't a museum in the world that's invulnerable" if the thief is clever and determined enough. The same probably holds for banks and other businesses. Those who have something valuable must consider a thousand small details that might make a theft possible; those who want to steal something need only find a few details that have been overlooked.

Unless human nature changes dramatically, there will always be great robberies, and those robberies will continue to make for fascinating news stories. We should resist the tendency to glamorize great robberies and the people who perpetrate them, however. What should never be forgotten is that while a great robbery might not directly harm specific individuals, all of society pays a high price when one of these crimes is committed. The thieves who pulled off the Gardner heist, for example, deprived everyone of the opportunity to view a dozen beautiful works of art. Then, too, people *do* sometimes get hurt or killed in the course of a great robbery, no matter how meticulously the caper has been planned. Those who are prepared to risk long prison sentences are often also prepared to harm anyone who gets in their way.

Bibliography

Baldauf, Scott. "Museum Asks: Does It Take a Thief to Catch a Degas?, *Christian Science Monitor,* August 29, 1997.

Behn, Noel. *Big Stick-up at Brink's!* New York: G. P. Putnam's Sons, 1977.

Bruns, Roger. *The Bandit Kings: From Jesse James to Pretty Boy Floyd.* New York: Crown, 1995.

_____. *Jesse James: Legendary Outlaw.* Springfield, N.J.: Enslow, 1998.

Conklin, John. *Art Crime.* Westport, Conn.: Praeger, 1994.

Crimes and Punishment: The Illustrated Crime Encyclopedia. Westport, Conn.: H. S. Stuttman, 1994.

Crimes of the 20th Century: A Chronology. New York: Crescent Books, 1991.

Delano, Anthony. *Slip-up: The Inside Story of the Wild International Hunt for the Last of the Great Train Robbers.* New York: Quadrangle, 1975.

Esterow, Milton. *The Art Stealers.* New York: Macmillan, 1966.

Fordham, Peta. *The Robbers' Tale: The Real Story of the Great Train Robbery.* London: Hodder and Stoughton, 1965.

Godman, David. "Art Attack: The Gardner Museum Heist." *Biography,* November 1998.

Illustrated World War II Encyclopedia. Westport, Conn.: H. S. Stuttman, 1995.

Lopez, Steve, and Charlotte Faltermayer. "The Great Art Caper." *Time,* November 17, 1997.

MacIntyre, Ben. *The Napoleon of Crime: The Life and Times of Adam Worth, Master Thief.* New York: Farrar, Straus, Giroux, 1997.

Mashberg, Tom. "Stealing Beauty." *Vanity Fair,* March 1998.

May, Robin. *The Story of the Wild West.* London: Hamlyn Publishing, 1978.

Morn, Frank. *The Eye that Never Sleeps: A History of the Pinkerton National Detective Agency*. Bloomington: University of Indiana Press, 1982.

O'Keefe, Joseph James. *The Men Who Robbed Brink's*. New York: Random House, 1961.

Read, Piers Paul. *The Train Robbers*. Philadelphia: J. B. Lippincott, 1978.

Ryan, Cornelius. *The Last Battle*. New York: Simon and Schuster, 1966.

Sayer, Ian, and Douglas Botting. *Nazi Gold*. New York: Congdon and Weed, 1984.

Settle, William A. *Jesse James Was His Name*. Columbia: University of Missouri Press, 1966.

Shand-Tucci, Douglass. *The Art of Scandal: The Life and Times of Isabella Stewart Gardner*. New York: HarperCollins, 1997.

Shirer, William L. *The Rise and Fall of the Third Reich*. New York: Simon and Schuster, 1960.

Weyermann, Debra. *The Gang They Couldn't Catch*. New York: Simon and Schuster, 1993.

Index

Index

Index

Picture Credits

Cover Photos   "Duchess of Devonshire" painting: printed with permission of Pinkerton Incorporated
Money: Photofest
Gold bars, picture frame: PhotoDisc

RICHARD WORTH has 30 years of experience as a writer, trainer, and video producer. He has written more than 25 books, including *The Four Levers of Corporate Change*, a best-selling business book. Many of his books are for young adults, on topics that include family living, foreign affairs, biography, and history. He has also written an eight-part radio series on New York mayor Fiorello LaGuardia, which aired on National Public Radio. He presents writing and public speaking seminars for corporate executives.

AUSTIN SARAT is William Nelson Cromwell Professor of Jurisprudence and Political Science at Amherst College, where he also chairs the Department of Law, Jurisprudence and Social Thought. Professor Sarat is the author or editor of 23 books and numerous scholarly articles. Among his books are *Law's Violence, Sitting in Judgment: Sentencing the White Collar Criminal,* and *Justice and Injustice in Law and Legal Theory*. He has received many academic awards and held several prestigious fellowships. In addition, he is a nationally recognized teacher and educator whose teaching has been featured in the *New York Times*, on the *Today* show, and on National Public Radio's *Fresh Air*.